JUST A JOB

THE RECOLLECTIONS OF COMEDIAN

NORMAN COLLIER

First published in the United Kingdom in 2009 by Mike Ulyatt
Enterprises, Willerby, East Yorkshire

ISBN 978-0-9561757-0-0

Printed in Great Britain by John Boland Print,
Churchill House, Churchill Street, Hull, East Yorkshire

The publishers have tried to trace and acknowledge copy-right holders,
but would be eager to rectify any omissions. Text copyright 2008 by

Norman Collier and Mike Ulyatt

ACKNOWLEDGEMENTS

Many thanks to: my son-in-law John Ainsley for pushing me to start
preparing these memoirs; Mike Ulyatt for helping me to recall details and
anecdotes and for preparing the manuscript for publishing; Hull Mail
News and Media and the Hull City Council Local Studies Library for
permission to use photographs from their respective collections;
everyone involved in the entertainment business who ever gave me a
job; finally, my wife Lucy and all my extended family for their loving
support over the years.
Norman Collier November 2008

Eric Sykes OBE CBE

FOREWORD

This is the most pleasurable long overdue tribute to a man I have admired for ages. Even as I write the name Norman Collier I am smiling, and as more memories of his extremely funny comedy creations spring to mind I'm chuckling, soon I'll be laughing outright and as I'm alone I'll be a sitting duck for the men in long white coats.

What is it about Norman that puts him in the comedy premier league, it's not his patter...it's his lack of it. For example when he makes his first entrance upstage as a cockerel, no fancy costume, just an ordinary lounge suit, flapping the arms of his jacket, head jerking curiously up down and sideways as if affronted by the untidiness of his domain, moving suspiciously on spindly legs placing each foot delicately to avoid treading on his breakfast.

How can anyone write for an artist of such high quality...all he has done is make an entrance onto a completely bare stage but to the audience it's a chicken run we can almost smell the droppings and here is another example. Countless wannabees have walked on to a stage endeavouring to emulate Norman's dodgy microphone routine but no one to my knowledge has had the talent to duplicate "The Cockerel".

I once sat in a restaurant with Norman which turned out to be a high speed lesson in humorous improvisation...I soon realised a well laid table is his prop room and in his eyes every object assumes another identity. For instance a fish knife becomes a cut throat razor which is expertly handled as he pinches his face into shavable proportions and after wiping the blade clean on the serviette he checks his reflection in a soup spoon, satisfied he picks up a plate and steers himself uncertainly through an imaginary snarl up. One episode followed another without a break and I'm sure a vase of flowers got in there somewhere. It was an evening I'll never forget but for the life of me I can't remember what he did next, in any case it was worth the cover charge.

Comedians over the years have tried to nick parts of Norman's act only to find when it comes to the test, their booty is worthless, it's like an expensive gift with the appendage 'Batteries not included...'

Norman Collier alone is the motivator.

1

Norman Collier

2009

It had been one of the most memorable moments of my show business career. I had just been introduced to Her Majesty Queen Elizabeth by the impresario Bernard Delfont on the night of the Royal Variety Command Performance which had been televised live from the London Palladium.I had done a six minute spot with plenty of visual gags and it had gone down pretty well with the audience and now I was stood in line with Bruce Forsyth, Tommy Cooper, Sacha Distel and Shirley Bassey together with everyone else who had been involved in the show and we were all to be presented to the Royal party backstage after the performance. I have no recollection what the Queen said to me or my reply but I do remember being introduced to Princess Anne and I bowed and shook her hand as we had all been instructed to do before the actual presentations started. I then committed the ultimate faux pas - I spoke to her before being spoken to first. In my act I had used quite a few hats and knowing of Princess Anne's penchant for them, I looked her straight in the eye and said, "Can I let you have some hats, Your Highness?" My intended quip totally backfired on me as she gave me a rather disdainful look and without saying a word to me, she moved onto the next person in line. Oh dear. I stood there on the thick pile carpet feeling very down in the mouth. I had been on a real high and now I was wishing a hole would appear in the floor and swallow me up. Would I be the first person from Hull to be incarcerated in the Tower of London?

Despite all the flashing cameras, the television lights and the general chatter, my mind began to wander. How on earth had a lad from Hull in East Yorkshire, with absolutely no early ambition to seek out a career in show business, ended up performing on stage before Queen Elizabeth and Princess Anne at the world - famous theatre, the London Palladium ? I was born in my Granny Dowling's house in Grotto Square Mason Street, Hull (or to give it its posh name, Kingston upon Hull) on Christmas Day, 1925 and weighed in at an enormous 15lbs 4oz. My dear mother Mary never walked in a straight line again and my dad Thomas Henry always reckoned that I should have been launched. Funny that I weighed so much, wasn't it ? I've hardly been above eleven stone dripping wet ever since and all the family, both on my mother's and my father's side, have only been of average build. We were a Roman Catholic family living in the centre of Hull and I was baptised at St Charles church in nearby Jarratt Street. It is a most beautiful church, built in 1828 and dedicated to St Charles Borromeo, Cardinal Archbishop of Milan and it was situated next to the premises of the Hull Brewery Company and the aroma from the brewing process was heavy throughout the area on a daily basis. It was a real working - class area and I was the eldest of eight children, five brothers and two sisters - Maurice, Peter, Bernard, Tony, Edward, Irene and Ann. Maurice emigrated to Australia in 1951 under the Government's £10 assisted - passage scheme and he died there in 2000 but his son Wayne has been over here to visit us several times and the rest of the clan still live locally. Big families were the norm in those days and my childhood memories of our family life together are all very happy ones. Dad worked as a builder's labourer and I remember him as a kind man with a quiet nature, around 5ft 7in tall with black, sleeked-down hair. Although we were happy and well-looked after, I can't really remember a lot of demonstrative love and affection within the family but maybe that was the way of the world then and you just got on with living. Our family was so poor that my dad used to make lavender bags for the gypsies to sell and when six of us went to the local fish and chip shop, we had to share a bag of chips between us and then spin a coin to decide who could drink the vinegar out of the bottom of the paper bag. Mum used to take the bones out of her corsets to make us all a stew and when my brother Maurice was born we had to share the same nappy as dad said it was the only way he could make ends meet! Dad had a black enamelled bike which he lovingly cleaned every Saturday morning in our back yard as mother would never allow him to bring the bike into the back kitchen because of the mess he might make on the canvas flooring. He fixed a saddle on the bike's crossbar for me and he took me all over on it - Hedon, Paull, Withernsea and Kilnsea-places which were ten to twenty miles away. The area around Hull is relatively flat and there were very few cars on the roads then so I always felt safe. We would take an empty jam jar and a wooden walking stick with a hook on the end which dad could use for collecting brambles from the hedges. He would then put the brambles into the jam jar and cover it with a brown paper bag and put it into his leather saddle bag and when we eventually arrived home, Mum would bake some delicious bramble pies for us, topped with hot custard. Mmm. Delicious. I can still recall the smell in our tiny kitchen. I always enjoyed the bike ride to Withernsea on the east coast. What excitement I felt when the lighthouse came into view and the anticipation of a paddle in the North Sea and perhaps an ice cream cornet. In later years, I became aware the jazz trumpeter Kenny Baker and film actress Kay Kendall had been brought up in the seaside resort. We did move house quite a few times, paying rent for properties which were all in the vicinity of the River Hull which separates the east and west sides of the city --- New George Street, Marvell Street and then Chapman Street. We never seemed to have much furniture or belongings to take with us and dad would pile all our wordly goods onto a wooden handcart and make several trips to our new residence, sometimes helped by a couple of my uncles. He would hire the handcart for 3d for half a day or 6d for the full day and we all had to help sweep it clean and then hose it down as it had to be returned in the same condition as when we took it out otherwise there was an extra penny to pay. It was too expensive to hire a chimney - sweeper so Mum would put some salt onto newspapers in the fire grate and put a match to them which blew the soot down from the chimney and then that had to be cleared up. Monday was always washday and everything stopped for that. The smell of carbolic soap still reminds me of the start of the week and our washing pegged to the washing line and flapping away in the back yard.

I started school at the age of five, firstly at St Gregory's, then St Mary's in Wilton Street between Dansom Lane and Holderness Road where the Sisters of Mercy nuns taught and they ran the school under a strict regime of discipline. I must admit I never liked school at all. I was a biggish lad for my age with bright red hair and I was bullied a lot with comments such as, "Now then Ginger" and "Ginger, you're barmy, you ought to join the army" and other insulting names including ginge, carrot-top, red head and beacon bonce. Looking back, I am sure that I tried to counteract this form of bullying by trying to make everyone laugh. Teachers used the cane on us kids on a regular basis, especially on a Monday morning at class assembly if you owned up to missing Mass on the Sunday morning. I did join the St. Mary's boxing club and I remember Chief Inspector Johnny Miller of Hull City Police taking a very keen interest in the club whenever his police duties allowed but my heart was never really in boxing, especially if I received a bloodied nose. It was always my intention to make people laugh but a lad named Slim Coghill who sat in the desk alongside me obviously did not agree with my philosophy and was always threatening me with his fist under the desk where the teacher couldn't see and whispering, "I'm going to get you after the bell tonight, Collier" and I got so fed up of these continuous threats that one afternoon I rose to his challenge and agreed to meet him for a fight in the nearby Dansom Lane public playground straight after school that day. Word soon spread around the school and a crowd of boys and girls followed the two of us , shouting out, " Fight, fight." Coghill soon laid into me and sat on top of me in the sandpit." Have you had enough yet, Collier ?" he shouted and for some unknown reason I answered, " no, let's go to St Mark Street "and we ran some 200 yards and grappled on the grassy bank of a drain before we tumbled down to the water's edge and I pushed his head under the dirty water, dragged him up and asked him if he had had enough and to my great surprise he said yes and that was that, we both went home for our teas. Slim never bothered me again, in fact we become good friends. Two other boys in my class, Tommy Wilson and his pal Weaver, challenged me to fight either one of them but I'd had enough of violence and I retired from fighting undefeated! I loved school sports days, especially the tug of war when I was usually the anchorman because of my size and Dennis Chapman and I regularly won the three - legged race and we both competed for top place in the high jump.

I moved schools to St Charles in Pryme Street but I still disliked all forms of learning. Our history teacher was Mr Steve Angold and he kept a short cane in his back pocket and I think it must have had my name engraved on it because I was always being caned by him. "Let me get my gun, Collier "he would say with a gloating look on his face. I am sure he enjoyed inflicting pain on his pupils, especially me and I was caned so often in school that my parents bought me a cane-bottomed chair to sit on at home! I remember being embarrassed at having to wear short trousers even though I was now thirteen years old. I had red, knobbly knees which I was very self - conscious about and I tried to hide my embarrassment by taking a pair of my dad's old trousers from his wardrobe and I dyed them dark blue and then I would change into them in a derelict house in Raywell Street each morning on my way to school and then change back on my way home after school finished for the day. This lasted for a couple of months before my parents bought me long trousers but thank goodness no one ever saw my antics. My parents bought me a secondhand bicycle, bright red it was and it was my pride and joy. I enjoyed free - wheeling down the slope after crossing the Chapman Street bridge over the River Hull when the frame of the bike suddenly snapped and I went head over heels over the handlebars but fortunately I escaped with only cuts and bruises. "Serves you right for cycling too fast" said my mam as she dabbed iodine ointment onto my leg and arm wounds and boy, did that sting - it brought even more tears to my eyes. Around this time I was taken into the Hull Royal Infirmary in nearby Prospect Street in the early hours of the morning and it must have been serious because evidently I was on the danger list for some time and I later found out that I had contacted diptheria from my brother Maurice.

There was an abbatoir near to the Railway Dock in Hull, just behind the Ellerman Wilson Line shipping offices and dad would often take me there. He wanted to see what went on but he never let me see the cows and sheep being killed although he would describe the bolt being put through the poor animal's head as we stood near the door. Perhaps my dad thought it was educational!

My pals and I always looked forward to the start of Hull Fair week at the beginning of October each year. It was held on a big site in Walton Street and said to be the largest travelling fair in Europe. I vividly remember the flashing bright lights, all colours of the rainbow and the noise of the rides, the showmen's raucous voices and the many different smells of food, hot chestnuts and sweets on offer but most of all, the hustle and bustle of the hundreds of people walking round the fairground. Joe Barak from Leeds was known throughout fairs in the north of England as CHICKEN JOE. "I'm the man you all know" was his boast and he ran a stall which offered carrier bags full of food items as prizes - cocoa, tea, lard, sugar, butter, jam and suet - all luxury items in the 1930's and beyond but his main prize offer was a plump, plucked, oven - ready chicken which was something we could only look forward to at Christmas. You bought a penny raffle ticket and if your three digit number came up on the lit - up number board then you won a chicken. What a showman the man was and people today still remember Chicken Joe. I always tried to win mam a bar of chocolate on the roll-a-penny stall but my efforts were usually unsuccessful and I ended up buying her one from the shop on the way home. The boxing booth fascinated me, four or five rough looking characters in white towelling robes stood on a rostrum while a showman issued a challenge of £1 to any man who could last three two - minute rounds with one of the boxers in the ring beyond. Not many challengers lasted the three rounds! There were coconut stands (did anyone ever knock one off its wooden stand?), the world's tallest man, the flea circus, the sheep with two heads, the tiniest woman you had ever seen, the hall of mirrors with its distorted shapes, the circus, the motorcycle wall of death, the shamrock ride, dodgem cars, hel-ter- skelter tower, the ghost train and the fortune teller where there was always a queue of people, mainly women, outside of their caravan homes but even then the fortune tellers were not always happy. I once asked how business had been. "Terrible "she replied, "if I'd known it was going to be as bad as it has been then I wouldn't have come." After all the fun of the fair, time to walk the two miles home with fish and chips from Bob Carver's mobile stall.

When all the fairground trucks had left after a week's fun, it was time to start planning for Bonfire Night, November 5th. We would make a scare-crow - type effigy of Guy Fawkes and place it on a bogey which was basi-cally two pairs of old pram wheels with a large plank of wood tied to them and our gang would wait outside of the Old English Gentlemen public house at the top of Mason Street and implore night - time drinkers staggering out of the pub to "spare a penny for the guy, please sir" and with the money collected we would buy some fireworks for the big night -

rockets, squibs, roman candles, catherine wheels and bangers - and we would also build-up a bonfire in the middle of the street with any wood or combustable material we could find. The hardest job then was to try to stop any rival gangs from setting fire to it before the big night while the fire-men from the nearby Worship Street Fire Station were not our greatest fans as they put out our bonfire on November 5th before it set fire to any of the adjoining houses. Rockets were put into empty jam jars to launch them as we ignored the printed warning on the rockets to " light blue touch paper and retire ". No Health and Safety Act in operation in those good old days. The morning after, as we made our reluctant way to school, we would poke the fire embers with a stick and hope to relight it and used rocket sticks would be collected, what for I have no idea now. I did play truant a lot from school, unbeknown to my parents I am ashamed to confess and my favourite haunt was the area around the Victoria Timber Dock which has been filled in and is now the site of a newish housing development. I would play among the timber floating in the dock pond. My parents would have gone mad if they had found out, especially as I couldn't swim a stroke. I would also collect empty beer bottles, usually the Hull Brewery brand, which the dockers had left after a liquid lunch break and I used to take the bottles to the nearest beer - off (off - license shop) and collect one old penny for every bottle returned to be used again by the brewery and that was a lot of money for me in those days.

After the excitement and unseen dangers of bonfire night, we could all look forward to Christmas, school holidays and snow. My mam and dad never had much money to spend on us but I can recall the anticipation leading up to Christmas, more so because December 25th was also my birthday. Early to bed on Christmas Eve and waking up in the dark, "Has he been yet, dad?" "we would all shout excitedly. "No he hasn't, get back to sleep all of you" was his usual answer. It always worried me that I would come downstairs on Christmas morning and find the stockings which we had hung up above the fireplace the night before would have been burnt to embers from the heat of the fire. Fortunately, that never happened and we usually found an apple, orange, sweets, a game of ludo or snakes and ladders and a shiny new penny in our stockings and we were all well satisfied with our lot AND I had a birthday cake to look forward to.

I can't really remember much about our relatives. Grandad John was a master baker at the local Co-op so we always had enough bread and cakes on the big day to go with rabbit or duck for Christmas dinner. My dad's mother was bed - ridden and we didn't see much of her at all but three of my uncles - George, Wilf and Alan - were good fun, particularly at our Christmas parties although they once took me to Holderness Road swimming baths and threw me in at the deep end. I don't know how I clambered out but it certainly put me off learning how to swim for the rest of my life. My Auntie Mona and Auntie Vera were always very good to me, well at least they laughed at all my jokes although they didn't reckon much to my singing, especially when I was Christmas Carolling around our street. I enjoyed it but more often then not our knocking on doors in hopeful anticipation of some dosh was met with the bang of a boot being thrown at the inside of the door and a loud voice shouting out, "bugger off home." Never a very profitable episode of our young lives, I'm afraid.

The firm of Reckitt's was founded in Hull and their premises were in Dansom Lane in the east of the city. Hundreds worked there and just before Christmas each year the philanthropic management put on a big party for the area's kids, It was held in a large hall with a huge, decorated Christmas tree in one corner and long trestle tables with white table cloths and plates of mince pies, Christmas cakes, sausage rolls, pork pies, chicken and turkey sandwiches. What a feast and did we kids look forward to it. Colourful decorations were hung across the hall and to end a perfect afternoon, we all received a goody bag from Father Christmas whose appearance in his red suit and big, white beard always brought a big cheer from us all. The goody bag contained fruit, sweets and a new sixpenny coin. I think the Reckitts family were Quakers, They built a Garden Village for their workers a short distance from the factory and offices and they really looked after their staff. The company manufactured starch for stiffening shirt collars and steradent to soak your false teeth in — funny mixture of things to make, wasn't it? Good job both were made in separate factories!

Saturdays were always busy days for me throughout the year. Errands to local shops for food in the morning and confession at St Charles at tea time. In the afternoon I was off to Queens Hall in Fountain Road with a big metal jug and glass basin to be filled with gravy and stew - one of the benefits of being part of a large family was that mam was entitled to some free food for us all. After taking that home and devouring my share, I was then off to Kress and Wagner Butchers opposite the Alexandra Theatre for savoury penny ducks which were a sort of square meat section in gravy and they tasted delicious warmed up. Teatime and after confession it was off to Fields Cafe in King Edward Street in the city centre to buy stale confectionery on offer before the shop closed for the weekend and then I would run to the Market Hall in the old town area. It was a huge building with white glazed brick wall tiles and sixty four open stalls, butchers shops and a large area for dairy produce and my favourite, Gohl's sweet stall. Birds Butchers would auction off meat until late on a Saturday night and there would be crowds of people bidding. I was always pleased to go home with my food bargains and felt proud that I was helping to feed the family each week.

Looking back, what a lot of characters were around Hull in the 1930's. Regular visits from the. scissor man" who had adapted his bike so he could run a sandstone wheel and water by pedalling, having raised the cycle's back wheel on a stand and he would sharpen knives and scissors and it must have been a worthwhile business because he was always busy. Gypsies often knocked on our door, selling wooden pegs for pegging out washing on the clothes line or "lucky lavender" and even offering to read your palm and tell your fortune in return for a silver coin. We had an insurance man who called every Friday night after tea and mam paid him sixpence to insure something or other, The man's name was Mr Sigsworth and he had quite a prominent nose. Before he came one night, mam said to us all, "Don't mention Mr Sigsworth's big nose because it's not very polite." Of course we couldn't resist the challenge and when he came into the house, one of my brothers piped up, "Don't worry Mr Sigsworth because we won't be mentioning your big nose." My dad was one of life's characters, a bit eccentric I suppose. He loved horse racing and he would scour the racing newspaper and place small bets with the bookies runner who would take them to his boss - betting shops were illegal in those days. I don't know if mam knew about dad's betting habits but I very much doubt it although he wasn't very successful anyway — a bit like father, like son! Thirty fights Johnny Duffy was an ex-boxer who would stop you in the street and forever tell you, "I had thirty fights in the square ring, you know." It always made good sense to listen and humour him and agree with his statement but Johnny never caused any real trouble and neither did another chap who must have been around forty years old but he was always dressed in short trousers and wore a schoolboy's red cap and he would run up and down our street, slapping his backside with his right hand and shouting," Hi, Ho Silver " and imitating his favourite cowboy character. Eva Smith was a well - known character in my later life, invariably appearing before the Stipendiary Magistrate at Hull Guildhall to be charged with being drunk and disorderly and ordered to spend a night in the cells but it never seemed to stop her doing it again. A chap named Martin Down only had one leg and he had a Union Jack flag strapped to his wooden stump and he rode a bike with only one pedal and he free-wheeled down the cobbled Charles Street on a fixed wheel. Every Saturday morning a "rag and bone " man would push his wooden handcart down the street and exchange an empty jam jar with a small goldfish swimming in water, a penny whistle or a windmill toy for any woollen garments. I have often wondered where the term "rag and bone" originated from and what it actually meant. I can remember a Mrs O'Neill in Mason Street. She baked hot cakes and mushy peas in her large kitchen oven and she would put them in a cardboard box and sell them from the front of her house. The butter oozed out of the hot cakes and really made you eager to buy, especially on a cold day but it all ended when she accidentally set her house on fire after hot fat from the oven dropped on the canvas flooring in the kitchen and the house was burnt down so that was the end of her little enterprise. "Penny a ride, penny a ride" called the man in a black, open wagonette pulled by a tired - looking horse but what a treat it was when we could afford it to sit in a horse - drawn carriage and we pulled faces at everyone we passed on the twenty minute ride. When we lived in Chapman Street, my dad worked as a dustman at the Hull Corporation refuse yard which was right opposite our house. Every morning, just before he left the house to go to work, he would look in the mirror in the room, adjust his cap and ask mam, "Anymore tea left in the pot, Mary?" "you'll be late for work if you don't hurry up "replied mam and this was a little ritual which happened on most workdays. Once when mam was in hospital after the birth of one of my brothers, dad was head cook and bottle washer and he decided to bake some Yorkshire Puddings for our Sunday lunch but he used whitewash instead of flour - well, it was the same colour, wasn't it? What a foul taste.

I was born in my Granny Dowling's house in Grotto Square, Mason Street, Hull on
Christmas Day 1925

Osborne Street in Hull, directly opposite was the butcher's shop where I started work as a
delivery boy in 1941

We lived in Chapman Street and later moved to Lockwood Street (below), both in central Hull

HMS Collingwood, Portsmouth 1943. I am third from the right, third row from the front

The American Frigate INGLIS.

Hello sailor! Me on board the aircraft carrier HMS TROUNCER during the Second World War

Our Wedding Group 28 August 1948.

My dad Thomas Henry and my wife Lucy on the beach at Withernsea.

Lucy and I spent our honeymoon in Southend in 1948. Check out the brogues I am wearing

My mother Mary holding my son Victor outside our home in Lockwood Street, Hull in 1950.

Tuesday 25th July 1950. A concert at the Dixons Arms in Woodmansey. I did a volunteer spot on stage on a night out with the darts team of my local pub, the Lockwood Arms,......Singing "We'll gather lilacs", in Soprano!!!

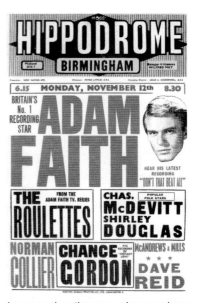

I appeared on the same show as singer Adam Faith at the Hippodrome Birmingham in 1962

My wife Lucy with our children Victor, Karen and Janet enjoying a day on the beach in 1961.

I appeared alongside singer Ronnie Hilton at Bridlington in 1974.

Vocalist David Whitfield and Reg Williams of Hull's Ambassador Club with the Bernard Delfont Award and television comedy award of 1971 presented to me by 'Michael Aspel' for BBC TV's "Ace of Clubs."

Dad said it was a genuine mistake but I had my doubts and I think he played a practical joke on all of us. Dad would often take us to the nearby Cleveland Cinema, usually just two of us because of the cost I suppose, then we had to wait another month or so for the next treat. Cowboy films were my favourites with cartoons a close second, all in black and white, of course. At the end of the films the National Anthem was always played and dad would take off his cap and stand to attention. One night a fork and ration book fell out his cap! As I was the oldest in the family, I was often left in charge of everyone if mam and dad wanted a night out together, I would get down on all fours in the room and let the kids sit on my back, one at a time and I would scramble round, shouting "Feed the horse, feed the horse " and the rider would pop pieces of chocolate into my mouth but when mam and dad came home, they would all accuse me of stealing their sweet ration, Later on, I would make a tent of bedclothes in our bed, tying the sheets to the four iron bedsteads and then I would tell my brothers and sisters stories in the dark which I made up as I went along — Willie the Worm, the Woman who Lived in a Kettle and Billy the Beetle were just some of the stories. Dad would sometimes stand at the bottom of the staircase, listening to my tales and then he would make ghost noises to frighten us all and it usually worked, more so if it was windy outside and the windows rattled in their frames.

We moved house once again, this time to number 22 Lockwood Terace in Lockwood Street and near to Wincolmlee. It was a two-up, two-down terraced house (two bedrooms upstairs and a living room and kitchen-scullery downstairs). The front door led into a narrow passageway with a staircase and at the back of the house was a small concreted yard with a toilet and coal house outbuildings and a wooden door leading out into a narrow" back alley" which linked all the houses. Ten of us slept in the two bedrooms. No hot water inside, only a cold tap and sink and water had to be boiled warm in a pan on the gas oven. Our immediate neighbours on either side of the house were the Coles and the Wilsons. Directly opposite our terrace was the Cannon Street Railway Station which was the terminus of the Hull and Barnsley Railway. I believe that there had once been plans for it to become Hull's main railway station but this never materialised. We were also near to the Barmston Drain which ran alongside the railway line for a short distance and past the big electricity station on Sculcoates Lane where hot water was regularly pumped into the drain and that made it a popular place for swimmers. How they did not contract typhoid or some other dreadful disease I will never know. Perhaps regular swimmers developed an immune system to the dirty water. Holidays away from home as a family were practically non-existent for us as we had very little money to spare. Trips to East Park and Pearson Park in the city were always enjoyable, especially fishing in the lakes for tadpoles and sticklebacks. Football and cricket matches were fun and the various swings and roundabouts in the play - area got some hammer from us. We all had a fear and a healthy respect of "Parky", the park attendant whose job it was to keep things tidy. Most Sunday evenings in the summer a brass band would play in the bandstand at Pearson Park and if the weather was fine everybody would turn up in their Sunday best and sit and listen. The real thrill for us though was a day trip by steam train to Withernsea or Hornsea, seaside towns some twenty miles from Hull. Excited kids with sandshoes freshly whitened would throng Hull Paragon Railway Station on a Sunday morning. Sandwiches and bottles of lemonade carried in brown paper carrier bags by parents and we were packed into tiny compartments on the train with no corridors. We counted off the stations on the way to Withernsea-Botanic, Stepney, Southcoates, Marfleet, Keyingham, Ottringham, Patrington and then the famous white lighthouse came into view - "We're nearly there "was the cry as we all tried to look out of the carriage window. The station at Withernsea was the terminus and a turntable alongside the main road was used to turn the engine round for its return journey to Hull, that was after it had been uncoupled from the carriages. We would watch that with great interest and then it was down the two hundred yards or so to the beach, sometimes stopping to buy an icecream or a tin bucket and spade. The beach always seemed to be crowded and I remember once dad had left us to buy a pot of tea for him and mam from a nearby stall and when he returned with the tray, he couldn't find us at first because of the crowds of people. Mam and dad would hire deckchairs for the day and me and my brothers and sisters would build sandcastles or go for a paddle in the North Sea which was always freezing and the pebbles and shingle would numb our feet as we ran back shivering to dry ourselves and then try to eat our sandwiches without getting sand in them - a real art, that was. If it rained we would all troop into the amusement arcades with our pennies, trying to win bars of chocolate or some novelty from the machines. Rock Bob was a big favourite of mine - a big stall on the seafront which stocked every type of rock sweet you could imagine and we would suck on the rock on the journey home, although more often than not we would all fall soundly asleep at the end of a very hectic day, only waking up when the train shuddered to a halt at Paragon Station and we began the short walk home.

2

Norman Collier

2009

I left school at 14 with absolutely no regrets at all and I think the teachers at St Charles RC School were relieved to see the back of me. My first job was in Mr Williams' greengrocers shop in John Street. Every Tuesday and Friday mornings he would send me to buy fruit and veg from the farmers and market gardeners wholesalers at Corporation Field in Park Street, later to be the site of Northern Foods offices and now a Tesco carpark, I had to load all the fruit and veg onto our wooden handcart and push it back to the shop. I once had a problem when the cart tipped over in Charles Street and cabbages, spuds, tomatoes, lettuces, carrots, rhubarb, spring onions, cauliflowers, radishes and oranges rolled all over the place which certainly didn't please the Hull Corporation busdriver behind me although to be fair, his conductor got off the bus and helped me pick everything up before it was nicked!

About this time the Second World War started and it became a big adventure for us as we collected shrapnel from the many bombs which fell near to our house. We lived in a largely industrial area, near to a strategic railway line, an electricity station, gas works and the docks so we were heavily targeted by German bombing raids and although many of my friends were evacuated to surrounding villages for safety reasons, many families decided to risk staying in their own homes. A brick air-raid shelter with a concrete roof was built in the middle of our terrace by Hull Corporation workmen and it had a wooden door entrance, whitewashed walls and bunk beds up to the ceiling on one side. I can still recall the eerie sound of the wailing air raid siren which pierced the night air, prior to another bombing raid and that seemed to happen most nights in 1941 and

1942. The parachute mines were the worst because you could hear them flapping in the wind as they dropped. I was out one evening with my brother Maurice and we both heard the dreaded flapping above us and we both threw ourselves on the pavement, clutching each other tightly and waiting fearfully for the explosion but fortunately for us, it exploded some distance away with no casualties. In the house we sometimes sheltered in the cupboard under the stairs instead of going to the shelter which wasn't a very clever idea considering the gas meter was installed there! One night as we all filed into the air raid shelter half asleep with dressing gowns over our pyjamas, mam dashed back into our house, ignoring the wailing siren." Where are you going, Mary "shouted our dad. "Back for my false teeth" was mam's muffled reply. "Come back here, the Germans are dropping bombs, not ruddy meat pies" my dad answered as he pushed us all into the shelter. Someone would always start singing during these nights and everybody joined in as it probably helped to ease the tension but with candles flickering throughout the shelter, it always seemed to me to be like a church service. Woe betide anyone who pushed open the door of the shelter to see what was going on during a raid when the firewatchers outside would admonish, "Put that light out, don't you know there's a war on?" All we wanted to do was to go to sleep in the bunk beds which we usually did despite the shelter shaking whenever bombs dropped nearby. I suppose fright became a way of life, you just got used to it and if anything was going to happen it would happen to all of us together.

I started a new job at a Jewish butchers shop in Osborne Street where a lot of jewish people lived and there was a synagogue nearby. The shop owner was Mr Sammy Felstone but his real name was Boguslavsky. His wife was a large lady who carried a small leather satchel around her waist to collect customer's money in. They were both nice people and were very good to me. My job was to deliver kosher meat to jewish customers along the Anlaby Road. I soaked the meat in water and then wrapped it in greaseproof paper and wrote the name of the customer on the paper. I had a company bike with a large wicker basket on the front and I wore a balaclava and gloves on cold days with a thick coat and black boots. One of my customers had a weekly order for Vienna sausages which were a sort of pinkish red colour and I was about to deliver them when I needed a pee urgently so I propped the bike up against a garden fence and relieved myself behind a tree. Unfortunately for me, I hadn't propped the bike up very well and it fell over and my parcels of meat dropped out of the basket onto the road and before I could do anything about it, two big dogs ran off with the Vienna sausages in their mouths. It took some explaining to the customer and to Mr and Mrs Felstone. Chickens were kept in the small yard at the rear of the shop and the Chief Rabbi would come through the shop carrying a long black case which had a razor in it and he would take it out and slit the chicken's throat, soak them in water in a large metal bucket, pluck all the feathers off and then burn off the whiskers. One of my other jobs was to clean up the shop after closing time, taking up the duck boards and sweeping up the sawdust from the shop floor. Most times I picked up coins which Mrs Felstone or customers must have dropped and I put them in a jar behind the shop counter.

Hull was being severely bombed during this time. We were close to the German mainland and the Humber made an easy marker for their planes to fly down the river and drop bombs on the docks and industrial areas which were to the east of the city. Us Hullites have never understood why our city was always announced as a "north east coast town" in radio bulletins and newspaper stories. Was it wartime censorship? £1.5 million was spent on a building campaign to provide a variety of air raid shelters to provide protection for the citizens of Hull --- timber ones which were sandbagged for extra protection, indoor Anderson steel structures, communal shelters, street brick buildings and domestic brick shelters, usually built in gardens at the back of the houses --- in total over 40,000 of these various designs were constructed in the city. Despite this building programme, over 400 were reported killed in Hull on bombing raids on May 7th and 8th 1941 when 300 high explosive bombs were dropped on the city by German bombers and all in all there were 82 separate air raids recorded by Civil Defence volunteers during the six years of the war and 1200 people were killed and 85,000 buildings damaged or destroyed. My parents often told me after the war of the tremendous community spirit within the city, despite the incessant bombing raids and the general deprivation.

I started my third job in 1942 in Albert Draper's scrap yard and my weekly wage was £3/10/-. For that I had to separate iron railings from their concrete settings in the front garden walls of houses by using a 7lb sledge hammer and then acetylene cutting equipment and the scrap iron saved was supposed to go towards the war effort for manufacturing fighter planes and tanks. I was working down Brunswick Avenue one morning and the hammer head came off as I raised it and the thing flew through the house window. Whoops! The householder was not very pleased, as you can imagine, and the firm had to fork out for a replacement pane of glass. Later that same week, I was walking down Wincolmlee alongside the banks of the River Hull when the local bobby came up to me and asked me to help him move a dead horse from the road and over the boundary of his patch as he was just about to go off duty for two days and he didn't want to spend time recording the incident. The police box at the top of a nearby street had been recently demolished in a bombing raid and he would have had to walk a couple of miles to his headquarters to write out his report. I had to apologetically refuse his request as I had plenty of my own work to finish that day.

3

Norman Collier

2009

I also worked at Sam Allon demolition company and at the British Oil and Cake Mills with my dad before I decided to enlist in the Royal Navy in June 1943 when I was 17½ years old. I have no idea what prompted my decision as there was no tradition of the sea in my family. I didn't fancy the Army as I could never see myself actually killing someone in hand - to - hand fighting and I never even considered joining the RAF. All my pals and workmates were volunteering and it seemed the natural thing to do at the time. I bought a suit from my Uncle Bill for 10/-. It was light grey in a silky material and after I had paid for it, I discovered a small burn in the trousers probably caused by a cigarette. I also bought a black and yellow tie and I went to have a portrait photograph taken at the Cecil Studios on Anlaby Road which cost me 6d and I proudly gave a copy of the colour picture to my mam and dad. I reported for my medical in Chapel Street, much later to be the headquarters of local radio station BBC Radio Humberside above the Post Office. I was passed A1 and posted straight away to HMS Collingwood training school and then onto Portsmouth for gunner training and I became an AA3 gunner after more gunnery training at the Whale Island Gunnery School.

My first posting was to join the American frigate INGLIS in Londonderry Northern Ireland and I was with a great set of lads. After an enjoyable night out ashore, we were staggering back to the ship when I saw a donkey in a field, tethered up to a wooden fence. I untied it and walked it through a gate and then rode it back to ship and up the gangplank, much to the amusement of my shipmates. I tied the poor animal to my gun battery and fed it some carrots from the food locker on deck. Next morning the ship's captain exploded with rage when he saw the donkey and he immediately ordered all the ship's company on deck and told us in no uncertain terms that unless the person who had brought the donkey on board owned up, then all shore leave for the next two weeks would be stopped for everyone. What could I do? I stepped forward and the captain said, "I might have guessed it was you, Collier". An order to return the donkey to its owner and apologise and two weeks in solitary confinement was my punishment. My practical joking regularly got me into trouble and I soon lost count of how many spuds I had to peel as punishment. One afternoon I borrowed an officer's cap and pretended to be Jimmy the One (Petty Officer), giving out orders to my pals in a posh accent but not realising he was stood behind me and he certainly was not amused - the result was even more spud peeling duties. There were thirty sailors crammed into our small cabin area and I soon got used to sleeping in a hammock. I never took the daily tot of rum and preferred to swap it for the rating's shore leave pass and this was very handy when we docked in Hull's Victoria Dock and I could walk the couple of miles home, carrying a gas mask and scarcely believing my eyes when I saw the scale of the bomb damage in the city and then I would be greeted by neighbours down the terrace with the question, "Now then Norman, when are you going back?"

I served in Malta where we ran the gauntlet of U Boats in the Med to provide the islanders and the garrison with food, arms, fuel and equipment. The island itself is only 117 square miles and had a population of 275,000 which made it one of the most densely populated areas in Europe and their agricultural resources could only feed around a third of the population so it was vital ships got through on a regular basis. Valetta was the capital and we spent some leave there although we had to hide in tunnels and caves during the frequent bombing raids but it was a formidable fortress. We moved onto the North Atlantic run later and that was scary at times with the ever - present danger of being hit by German U Boat torpedos and having to contend with strong nor'wester gales, heavy snow and sleet storms, cloud, mist and fog and icing-up. I was on watch one night in absolute pitch black which was a very lonely time and the lookout on the bridge shouted out to the captain," Torpedos on the port side, sir "but fortunately for us it turned out to be two porpoises which appeared fluorescent in the dark and the sailors on watch breathed a big sigh of relief. I don't know if it was because I was so young, but I never remember being scared despite the great risk and loss of naval and merchant navy ships due to enemy action. Was it the sheer exuberance of youth? I have often received invitations to INGLIS reunions but they are not my cup of tea so I have never attended any. I'm happy with my North Atlantic Crossings medal, still in its presentation box, and thankful I came safely through the action. We still had some fun on board despite all that was going on. Lofty Evans was a good pal of mine but boy, did he snore when he was asleep. We decided to try to stop this and get some sleep ourselves so we released the knot on the feet end of his hammock and lowered it until he was in the upright position. He never once woke up during this and it did stop him snoring for a while. We once docked in Murmansk and three of us went on shore leave together. It was a cold, miserable place and a Russian lady, very thin and unkept and with two small children, was sat on a wall combing her dirty hair with a wooden comb. I turned round and went back on board ship and took a comb out of my bag and went back and gave it to her and she was very grateful for what was a luxury item to her. Returning to Belfast, we were loading stores on board as well as small "hedgehog" bombs and they had long spikes on them and they were fired in patterns forard of the ship and the scattered splinters of the bomb helped us to pick-off patrolling U Boats. On this particular loading day, my oppo accidently dropped one of the bombs on deck and I have never seen dockers move so fast as they did that day. On board, we were shown American films warning us what could happen if we got VD and other diseases but that didn't seem to bother some ratings. We once picked up six Germans in the Atlantic after their Dornier aircraft had been shot down. They had been in a liferaft for several hours and they were all covered in oil and shivering in the bitter cold despite the bulky clothing they had on. Our captain ordered them to be kept secure and they were locked up in the ship's laundry room. I later got chatting to one of them, a blonde lad called Peter and he showed me some photographs of his family back home in Berlin. He seemed like a good bloke to me but one of the other captured men was identified as a Gestapo officer and our Military police were waiting dockside when we sailed into Belfast harbour and they took charge of our unwanted guest. We moved onto sweeping the area between Lands End and the French coast, or so we thought, because we came under fire from enemy positions in France. In thick fog we had thought we were just off Lands End! I later served on the aircraft carrier TROUNCER in the Far East for several months and we were docked in Calcutta when news came through to us of the dropping of the H-Bomb in Japan which was to bring World War Two to an end and we joyfully sailed back to dear old blighty.

4

Norman Collier

2009

After nearly two and a half years service in His Majesty's Royal Navy, I was demobbed and returned home to Hull to a fantastic welcome, which was the same for all ex-servicemen and women throughout the entire country. Welcome home messages were painted on gable end walls and street parties and celebrations in the pubs and clubs were held to mark the end of hostilities. I remember walking out of Paragon Railway Station with my suitcases and staring open - mouthed at the amount of bomb damage - nothing remained of Hammonds department store and the city centre was practically all flattened. There was a sombre air in the city but for me, I was more than pleased to be safely home. After a couple of weeks trying to settle back into life on civvy street, I had to start looking for a job. I did seriously consider signing on in the Royal Navy for another seven years and I was actually halfway up the stairs to the recruiting office when I had second thoughts and I turned round and made my way to the Hull Corporation offices and registered as a labourer. With the whole of the city having suffered so much bomb damage to houses and buildings, the Corporation had started a massive re - building scheme and I was given a job straightaway as a general handyman, putting up scaffolding, repairing ceilings and attics and working on pre - fabricated bungalows. These were known locally as "prefabs" and they were intended to be temporary homes but some were still being lived in fifty years later. I moved on to being a bricklayer's mate on Corporation housing in north and west Hull and I was helping bricklayer Alf Copping to point up chimney stacks down Hawthorn Avenue when Alf said he was knocking off to go down to the local corner shop for a packet of five Woodbine cigarettes. I offered to go for him but Alf wanted to stretch his legs and off he went, climbing down the ladder. I took his trowel and continued the work of making the chimney stack safe and sound but unfortunately I accidentally dropped a brick down the chimney. Well, what a commotion developed. The lady of the house came out of the back door, looking up and shaking her fist at me as I peered down at her," Come down here, you ginger - haired *******, I'll wring your ****** neck" she shouted. I quickly clambered down the ladder and followed her back into the house and what a sight in the small kitchen -- the lady had been baking and on a square table were apple pies, lemon curds, jam tarts and custard pies, all covered in a thick, black layer of soot which had come down the chimney as a direct result of me dropping the brick. What could I do but profusely apologise although I did resist the naughty temptation to lighten up the moment by telling her that her baking looked well burnt!

I later worked on houses in Anlaby Road and Hall Road with Charlie Jacques who became a good pal but by the middle of 1947 nearly all of the re - building work by the Corporation was completed and I was out of work. The winter that year was a very hard one and there was a lot of snow and I was clearing all the snow from our terrace one day when a young lady walked by and smiled at me. WOW! Something electric passed between us, was it a milk float?! This was my first meeting with Lucy Seddon who lived at number 19 Lockwood Terrace. She worked as a machinist in Wilson's dress shop in Whitefriargate and she was very slim and attractive. I plucked up the courage to ask her for a date and she agreed. We later walked down to the Strand cinema on Beverley Road where we saw the Jolson Story. After that date we were inseperable and I bought a second hand tandem and we biked all over the place together.

We once went to Bridlington, a seaside town about thirty miles from our house and it seemed like a head wind all of the way there and although we stopped at a couple of cafes for a cup of tea, I was absolutely shattered by the time we got to Brid seafront and I am convinced to this day that Lucy put her feet up behind me and let me do all the hard work pedalling but she only laughs when I ask her about it.

I eventually proposed to Lucy and we were married in St Charles RC Church in 1948. Lucy was 19 years old and I was coming up to 23. My father gave Lucy away and my Uncle Jim was the best man. We held our reception in the church hall at St Saviours in Stoneferry. There were no stag nights or hen nights in those days. During the victory parade in London I had met up with a chap called John Verlander and we kept in touch, John's sister Margaret was married to Len Curtis and the couple ran a shoe shop in Southend and they very kindly invited us to spend our honeymoon there . We went down by train and stayed with a Mrs Snatchell who lived next door to Len and Margaret. They were very good to Lucy and me and they not only gave us a £10 note as a wedding present but they also paid for our accommodation. We stayed friends until Len died, aged 82. When we got back to Hull we lived with Lucy's mam and her step - father, Fred Billham and spent most evenings huddled round the coal fire, listening to the Redifusion radio. The house was right on the corner of the terrace and every fifteen minutes of the day, a Hull Corporation Transport number 30 bus went by and the whole of the house seemed to shake.

The three happiest days of our lives were when our children Victor, Janet and Karen were born. Victor came into the world on in August 1949 at the Hedon Road Maternity Hospital in East Hull and after ringing the hospital from the white telephone box at the top of our street and receiving the good news, I dashed out and embraced a passing neighbour with such joy, confiding in him, "It's a boy, it's a boy." He must have thought I was nuts. Janet was born at home in February 1951 when we had moved to live on our own down Arthur Street and Karen was also born in Hedon Road Maternity Hospital in February 1956. Lucy was brunette, Karen was fair while both Victor and Janet had auburn hair, like me. Victor is an excellent musician and we appeared on stage together many times and he now entertains locally just for the fun of it. Victor married Margaret in June 1973, Janet is married to Peter and they have two daughters, Rebekah and Jackie. Rebekah is married to Dave and they have a daughter, Lois. Jackie's partner is Pedro and they have two children, Jasmine and Marcos. Karen and John were married in June 1979 and they have three children -- Jonathan, Lucy and Thomas. Our children, grandchildren and great - grandchildren have given Lucy and I some great moments over the years. There are eighteen of us when all the family get together -- guess who ends up washing up after we have all eaten together?

But I digress. I had got a job as a general labourer at the Distillers Company Limited (DCL) at Saltend which is to the east of Hull. My duties were in the yard gang and I drove a small Lister three wheel vehicle, collecting scrapmetal from around the factory site. My starting wage was £7 a week which I could increase to £9 with overtime. It was hard work but I enjoyed it. I remember one incident very vividly. It was in the week leading up to a General Election in the country. I found a large, brass funnel in one of the yards and it was shaped a bit like an ice - cream cornet. As I drove the Lister around the yard with one hand on the steering wheel, I used the other hand to hold the funnel close to my mouth and shouted, "Vote for Collier in the Election, he won't let you down "and my voice echoed around the buildings. It brought loads of laughter from the lads but I thought I was in real trouble when Mr John Howlett, the company's top man, came striding purposefully across the main yard towards me. I stopped the Lister and put the funnel down. "What's your name?" he asked." Collier sir " I replied. "Right Collier, follow me" and he strode across to the drum shed, with me half running and half walking behind him. "Are you happy working here, Collier?" he asked. "Yesss sir" I stuttered in reply. Mr Howlett pressed the button which automatically opened the huge steel doors of the drum shed and when they were fully opened, he said to me, " What do you see here, Collier?" "Lots of men steaming and painting drums, sir" was my reply. " Yes, but what else?" "Well, nothing really, sir". Mr Howlett smiled. "Everyone has a smile on their face, Collier. You made them all laugh and that's good for morale and it keeps production going. Good man. Keep it up." With that, he walked briskly away, leaving me not only very relieved but also very happy that I was continuing my long term ambition to make people laugh.

Shortly after this episode, I went on a Saturday night out with my pal from our Hull Corporation workdays, Charlie Jacques and we ended up at the Perth Street Club which was known locally as "the dead centre of Hull" because of the cemetery right next to the place. We were both dressed up in our best suits, white shirts and bootlace ties. Most clubs then in Hull were privately owned, usually by local businessmen and management put on artistes for their members' entertainment on a Saturday and a Sunday and artistes were usually semi - professional. On that particular Saturday night a male singer from Goole had been booked to perform two spots of about thirty minutes each. The club's concert secretary was Fred Pine and one of his many duties at the club was to introduce the evening's performer but just after Charlie and I had arrived and with the clubroom nearly full with around 100 people sat at tables or stood chatting at the bar, Fred climbed up onto the small stage and announced over the tannoy system, "Ladies and Gentlemen, I'm sorry to have to tell you that tonight's act has had a blowout (puncture) at Howden so he's not going to be able to be with us this evening. Now do we have any volunteers in the audience who fancies doing a turn to entertain us tonight?" A loud, collective groan greeted Fred's announcement. I had just got Charlie and myself a drink at the bar when he pushed me forward. "This lad will tell a few funnies" he told Fred, who was very relieved that he had at least one volunteer for the night. The club's pianist was Flo Smith and I asked her to play WE'LL GATHER LILACS IN THE SPRING which I sang in a soprano voice and alternated in a deep voice. I then did impressions of Churchill, Montgomery and Hitler, sang something by the American group The Inkspots, told a few gags and finished with a take-off of Family Favourites which was a popular radio show on the BBC at the time and it was broadcast on a Sunday lunchtime with record requests. All in all, I did about twenty five minutes and at the end I received a grand reception and I think Fred bought me a pint as a thank you, Flo asked me if I was an artiste and I thought she meant did I paint. She thought I was pulling her leg when I told her it was my first-ever appearance on a stage but she was very helpful and suggested I go to the next meeting of the Hull Artistes Federation at the Hull Young People's Institute on George Street the following Monday evening when prospective club acts were given a five minute audition. A Mr Bird was Hon Sec of the Federation and he introduced acts who did their thing in front of a committee of three or four sat at a long table in front of a stage. They listened to your act and decided collectively if they considered you to be good enough to appear in local clubs, I must have made a good impression because I was immediately invited to join the Federation. It cost 5/- and I received a little red book with my name and address in it and their rules and regulations, I suppose it was a kind of Equity card and without it you were not allowed to work in local clubs as a performing artiste, Every month club concert secretaries and artistes would meet up socially at the Ambassador Club on Holderness Road and the secretaries would book acts to appear at their clubs for the following month, depending on what fee the artiste was asking for and if that figure was in the club's entertainment budget. A fair bit of haggling over these fees usually went on before a firm handshake between secretary and artiste agreed terms to be paid on the appearance night and both then entered the date in their respective diaries.

5

Norman Collier

2009

The clubs themselves were workingmen's clubs and were the heart and soul of the local community and most areas in Hull had their own club, usually converted from houses and sparsely furnished with brown or green walls plus a bar dart board and snooker table. Changing rooms for the artistes were practically non - existent and most came ready changed to do their spot on stage. Car parks were not needed as people walked the short distance to their local club. Some clubs in the really poor areas of the city used beer crates as extra seating and the snooker table would be covered over to allow members to stand their drinks on it without marking the cloth. They all seemed to me to do a good business and clubs generally featured a singing act or a comedian on a Saturday and Sunday evening with some putting on a striptease act on a Sunday lunchtime. Strict licensing laws meant any advertising of these female acts on posters or in the local press had to be shown as "exotic dancers" and my sympathy always went out to comics who worked on stage immediately before the girls came on as they were usually on a hiding to nothing because all the lads in the audience had only come to see the striptease act. Everyone had to be a member of the club and pay a small annual subscription and agree to abide by club rules. Non-members had to be signed in by a member as a bona fide guest and the local police would often raid a club without warning and check off those present against the club's register and some clubs ended up being struck off and refused a liquor licence and had to re - apply for a licence because they had not followed the city's strict licensing laws. One big advantage of belonging to a club was that the drinks were cheaper than those in public houses. Most clubs also ran an annual outing to the theatre pantomime at Christmas and an outing by coach to the seaside in a summer. These were for the children of club members and each child went free of charge with perhaps a gift of half a crown to spend on sweets or ice cream. The Key family owned quite a few clubs in Hull and they certainly raised the standards by providing comfortable suroundings, food such as scampi and chicken in a basket and they brought in class acts from out of town for the benefit of their members. The Westfield Country Club in Cottingham, a large village just outside of Hull, was owned and run by the Brown family and was very popular in the 1960's and 70's when top quality entertainers featured on a weekly basis,

A favourite club of mine locally was Dee Street Club off Hessle Road which was in the heart of the city's fishing industry. It was owned by Wally Palmer and his family and they also owned other clubs in the area. Billy Carmichael was the club's concert secretary and 'Carmo' became a good friend to me although he would always haggle down to the last penny before reluctantly agreeing to my fee. One Saturday night at the club I did my usual three 40 minute spots to a full house and I went down a bomb with repeated requests for an encore, which I did. I went off stage into the small dressing room absolutely shattered when in came Carmo, "Do me another twenty minutes, please Norm. They're going mad for you out there "he urged. I groaned about having no more energy and not much more material left but I obligded, another 20 minutes and a standing ovation. He came in the dressing room, winked and said "squeeze us another one in". I gasped, "I've done over 2 hours. I don't know anymore songs". He promptly went to the audience and announced:- "Norman won't be back on, thats all he knows"!!!!. Wilf Nesfield owned the Inglemire Club in north

Hull and he was a nice man, encouraging me as I built up my act and making my way into show business. In later years, Wilf and I joined up with Joyce Clark as a trio and what good singers they both were and I suppose we were a sort of concert party and we did have some laughs, on and off the stage. The Transport Club in Lombard Street was home territory for off - duty drivers and conductors on Hull Corporation's blue and white buses. I was once halfway through my act there and I had two chairs on stage, going through my driving school routine. It was going down a lot better than normal with the audience but my self - confident mood was nipped in the bud when the club pianist came on stage and she whispered in my ear that my flies were undone, Quick exit, stage left but it got such a big laugh that I thought seriously about keeping it in the act. My first - ever official booking was at the Suttonway Club in Marfleet Lane, east Hull. The club was right in the middle of the Preston Road council estate and was a really popular venue on a Saturday night and I received the princely sum of 10/- (50p) for two fifteen minute spots. I can't recall being nervous at all before going on stage but I did some visual stuff and I enjoyed the experience. I had no great ambition to continue a career in local club land, never mind the wider enclaves of show business.

I met some great characters in Hull's club land life. Brian Winchester worked in the Hull Daily Mail advertisement department and he wrote an article about local club land news in the Hull Times, which was the Mail's weekly newspaper, published every Friday morning. Brian was also an accomplished club entertainer in his own right with a nice, easy style of singing, some zany gags and he also blew up balloons and bent them into some unusual shapes. Brian's wife Dorothy was a bridesmaid for us when Lucy and I were married. Johnny Rix would black up his face and do a sort of one man Black and White Minstrel Show and another act, Norman

Harrison, dressed up as Al Johnson and mimed to Jolson's records with his wife Dolly sat backstage operating their portable gramaphone. It was a well - rehearsed act and Norman was a popular entertainer. Not everyone in his audiences realised that his was a mime act and I nearly spoilt it for him one evening when I was sat at the back of the City Hotel in Hull's Old Town area, waiting my turn to go on stage when Norman had finished his act. A chap sat next to me said, " He's good, isn't he? He sounds just like Jolson." I had to tell him that it was actually the American singer he was listening to. "What! All these years I've been listening to Norman and I thought it was him singing. What a cheeky so-and-so." he replied. I wished I had kept quiet but it got even worse. After I had finished my act, Norman came back to do a second spot and he was miming to another Jolson recording as he came on stage and I walked off. Unfortunately, as I pushed the curtains back at the side of the strage, I didn't realise that Dolly was sat just behind them and I accidently bumped into her, only slightly but enough to knock her against the gramaphone which caused the record on the turntable to stick. I quickly went back on stage and started singing "April Showers" where Norman had left off and when Dolly had put the record back in the groove, Norman continued singing and I walked off stage for the second time that night. It was a funny moment but I don't think it fooled many people in the audience. Another of Norman's acts was miming to Frankie Laine's 'Mule Train' recording when he would bang a tin tray on the top of his head at the end of every chorus, so hard that it always gave me a headache, never mind him.

In the 1960's we were living at number 18 Eastmount Avenue, off Saltshouse Road in east Hull and I was continuing working at DCL while travelling to more and more out-of-town bookings on an evening. I could earn £65 most weekends in the clubs and I was seriously considering leaving the company and becoming a full - time professional but it was a big decision to make and I pondered what to do for best for a few months. I bought a 2 litre Vauxhall Wyvern in British Racing Green on hire purchase from Thompson Used Cars in Anlaby Road near to Hull city centre and it became my pride and joy. It also meant that I could get to and from clubs in South and West Yorkshire much more easily than travelling by train and taxis. Most times I hadn't been getting back home until 3am and that was no good for family life. I called at my mother's house shortly after I had bought the car. She was now a widow and I offered to take her out for a drive but I was a bit upset when she said, "No thanks, Norman. I don't want to get a draught down my neck." "But the car has windows in it mam", I protested but she was adamant and so that was that. The yard gang foreman at work was a Mr Hamilton and he had an old banger of a car and he couldn't understand how one of his men could have a better car than he had. I think he was a bit jealous and he started to give me some of the worst jobs on site --- cleaning toilets and other dirty jobs. The factory shut down completely for two weeks every summer and we had to clean out the boiler house which meant me and a character nicknamed 'Jack the Mole' stripped down to our underpants with mouth mask and goggles on and we worked in hot temperatures to bring out the accumulated ash. I decided there and then that enough was enough and I handed my notice in. It was a big step I had taken and I had no idea where my new career was to take me, all I knew was that I wanted to do what I had always wanted to do and that was to make people laugh.

In Hull in the early 1950's, David Whitfield and Ronnie Hilton began singing in local clubs. David had served seven years in the Royal Navy as a gunner like me and saw action on the battleship RAMILLIES on D-Day. I was just five weeks older than David and he lived in the Drypool area of

Hull before moving to Stoneferry, only half a mile across the River Hull from where I used to live in Lockwood Terrace. He was working for the Hull Concrete and Stone Company as a cement mixer before he turned professional and we were to become friends. We were once appearing as separate acts at the Buckingham Club in east Hull and David was billed as the "Singing Sailor" and we were chatting to each other in the club's committee room before getting changed when the club secretary opened a drawer in a locker and took out a brand new white pith helmet and told me I could keep it if it was of any use to me. David and I both did our acts on stage and at the very end of the evening I put the helmet on with a small Union Jack flag on top of its spike, picked up a long-handled brush to use as a pretend rifle and marched round the club singing 'Goodbye, Goodbye' as made popular by that great Irish tenor Josef Locke. Being the good sport he was, David came and joined me in a sort of duet and it went down so well with the club goers that I soon developed a routine round it, putting on a ragged vest and a pair of shorts with holes in and a topcoat, wore an enormous pair of black flippers, a wooden imitation rifle and of course the pith helmet with flag attached. I would then sing the songs ' On The Road To Mandalay' and 'Goodbye, Goodbye', accompanied by the club pianist and drummer and finished off by getting the audience to take out their handkerchiefs and wave them, above their heads while joining me singing. In later years, top comedian Ken Dodd did something similar in his act so I dropped it as I didn't want to be accused of copying a fellow comedian's act. David topped the bill at Hull's Tivoli Theatre in July 1953 and said to me, "Norman, I used to sit in the gods at theTivoli watching shows and never in my wildest dreams thought I would eventually appear on the stage there ." He went from earning 1O/- a night in local clubs to £300 a week after he had appeared on the Hughie Green Talent Show on Radio

Luxembourg and his singing career really took off. Hit record followed hit record --- Martha, I Believe (which went to Number 1 in the Hit Parade), Answer Me, Rags to Riches, Be My Love, The Street Where You Live, Santa Natale and Beyond The Stars. David's greatest hit record though was 'Cara Mia' which sold over three million copies and he became the first British singer to earn a Gold Disc which was presented to him at a David Whitfield Convention held in Blackpool's Winter Gardens He even named his new house in Kirkella in the suburbs of Hull 'CARA MIA' and his wife Sheila and son Lance were very proud of him as we all were. He later topped the bill at the Palladium, and starred on three Royal Command Performances and starred on the Ed Sullivan TV Show in America.

Charity work took up a lot of my time but I have always tried to help good causes. One such event was held at Gosforth Park near Newcastle and I was asked to do a thirty minute spot at the end of a charity golf day at the Matfen Hall to raise funds for a Sheltered Housing and Workshops project which was a north east based charity working with people with disabilities and it was part of a British Airways celebrity golf tour. The next lunchtime I was booked at a club at Redhouse and I was halfway through my act when a door at the back of the room was flung open and a small, bald headed guy called out to his pal sat at the front, "Hey Geordie, your pigeons are back" whereupon another guy in the audience stood up and shouted to the little man, "Are mine back yet?" and then practically everyone in the room piled outside to see if their blasted pigeons had returned to their lofts. One old chap remained sat at the front, smoking a pipe. I said, "Aren't yours back yet then, Pop?" " Nah, I keep whippets "he smiled and carried on smoking his pipe as I gathered up my props and admitted defeat.

I was doing pretty well in the 1960's as I got more and more out of town bookings although I always liked to get home after shows even if it was sometimes in the early hours of the morning. I was always a home bird, still am. There is something about the Hull area. My roots are here and the people are really great --- tough, and cynical but open and positively friendly. Before the opening of the M62 Motorway and the building of the Humber Bridge (once the longest bridge of its kind in the world), Hull was a very insular and parochial place, a sort of big little village. Entrepeneurs have flourished in the city over the years --- Reckitts, Needlers Sweets, Comet, Smith and Nephew, Ranks, Cattles, Priestmans, Humbrol, Ellerman Wilson, Hygena, Seven Seas and Northern Foods - all companies which were originally started up by local people. Celebrities such as Roy North, Ian Carmichael, John Alderton, David Whitfield, Ronnie Hilton, Freddy Sales, Maureen Lipman, Joe Longthorne, Amy Johnson, Roland Gift, Tom Courtenay, Debra Stephenson, Paul Heaton, Steve King, Pat Bredin, Barrie Rutter, Peter Martin and more recently Liam Mower; sporting personalities Jimmy Binks, Mark Robinson, Nick Barmby, Johnny Whiteley, Jack Hale, Mike Bore, 'Young' Con O'Kelly, Karen Briggs, Wally Mays, Ernie Hardaker, David Howes and David Oxley; playwrights Alan Plater and John Godber, politician John Prescott, world famous poet Philip Larkin and footballers Raich Carter, Dean Windass Ken Wagstaff and Steve Mclaren - all with Hull connections while William Wilberforce, the slave emancipator, was born down Hull's High Street and we even had our own telephone service once, run by the Hull Corporation under a licence from the General Post Office, We have a lot to be proud of in Hull and in 2008 Hull City Football Club was promoted to the Premiership for the first time in its 104 year history.

6

Norman Collier
2009

In the Spring of 1962 workingmen's clubs throughout Yorkshire picked top acts to appear in a show called 'Clubland Performance' at the Blackpool Opera House and I was delighted to be invited to appear, along with Dukes and Lee, Doreen Beales and Colin Crompton, The show was compered by Michael Aspel in front of a full house and afterwards Sydney Grace from the Grade Organisation came to my dressing room and asked me if I would like to join the Cliff Richard Show at the new ABC Theatre in Blackpool in the summer of 1963. The show was to be produced by Albert Knight and of course, I accepted the offer and he made me very welcome at rehearsals as did Cliff, Hank Marvin and the rest of the Shadows. Fellow artistes on the bill were that great ventriloquist Arthur Worsley (who always spoke directly to me through his dummy Charlie Brown), Daley and Wayne and Carol Gray. I was sat in the stalls one afternoon, watching Cliff and the Shadows rehearse, when two young lads came down the theatre aisle and sat next to me. 'Hello lads, what do you do?' I asked, just trying to make polite conversation. "We're in a group" replied one of them. 'Oh yes, what's the group's name?' I continued. "The Beatles like and we're from Liverpool, just up the road." "Well, that's a funny name for a group." What did I know, I only found out later that I had been chatting to George Harrison and Ringo Starr before their great fame.

I was only offered £60 a week but I never fully realised at the time how important this job was. I thought it was just a job but I will always be grateful to the Grade Organisation for giving me my big chance even though I still had no great ambition to make a lasting career in show

42

business. The show at the ABC started off with a film backdrop of Cliff and the Shadows in a car which ended in a crash and that was my cue to walk on stage to start my act. It proved to be very difficult to get any laughs following the film intro. I tried walking on stage with a tyre round my neck and another night I staggered on clutching a steering wheel, anything just to get a laugh but still little response from the paying customers. The Great Train Robbery was headline news in all the newspapers and on television and one of the robbers was nick named 'The Weasel' and a tabloid newspaper had offered a reward of £1000 for his capture and conviction. I came on stage singing, "Half a pound of two penny rice, half a pound of treacle, there's a £1000 reward, if you find the Weasel." That finally broke the ice and topicality had won the day and I had cracked it. Years later, Albert Knight admitted to my wife Lucy that he had always regretted giving me such a tough spot. The season lasted for sixteen weeks and I was on my way. Hyme Zohl was a London - based showbusiness agent, and he offered me a six month contract with the stipulation that I lived in London but after talking things over with Lucy, I turned it down. I was a northern comic with no wanderlust.

Work had began to pour in and I hardly had a night off during the next two years so I felt fully justified in making the decision not to move to the big city. A guy in dark glasses called Harry Gunn came to introduce himself after one of the performances at the ABC Blackpool. He was a theatrical agent and he offered to act as my sole manager and also to take care of my financial interests. I thought that it was the right time for me to have some form of representation so I signed a contact with Harry. His dark glasses earned him the nickname of 'The Welder' in showbiz circles. His office was part of his house in Sale, Cheshire

I began to develop more characters in my act and based my club secretary impressions on real life characters I met at venues such as Rotherham Trades and Labour Club and the Greaseborough Social and Welfare Club. They were usually small, dapper men with glasses and thinning hair, plastered down with Brylcreem hair cream, blue suit and tie with long cuffs on their white shirtsleeves. Probably they were hen pecked at home or bullied by their boss at work all week but come the weekend they were all - powerful at the club and woe betide any artiste who crossed them because they were soon cut down to size. "Now tonight's act is a comedian, so he says, so if you like laughing then you might enjoy him" was my introduction one night. Nothing whatsoever in Clubland was allowed to interfere with the bingo or raffle, they were both sacrosanct, while the arrival of the hot meat pies, mushy peas and sausage rolls was a highlight of the evening. The concert secretary would think nothing of taking the microphone off the artiste, even in the middle of a song or a gag, to announce to the club members, "Get your bingo (or raffle) cards in the next ten minutes . Tonight's jackpot special will be £50" or "Meat pies are here at back of room but hurry up, they won't stay hot for long." Never an apology to the act, you just had to carry on as though nothing had happened, More often than not, an artiste's fee was paid out in pound notes, by the Concert Chairman, grudgingly, with each note slowly laid out on a wet bar while the passing audience, bar staff and anyone who cared to watch saw your fee being paid. Someone would often say, "I had to work down t'pit all week for that much" My reply was, "I'm a Collier too, you know". A concert secretary came to me after I had done a lunchtime spot at his club and pointed at me with both thumbs up, saying "You'll do for me, Tommy." I had to laugh, Tommy Collier? I later told this story to Bobby Ball, who was then in a comedy duo called The Harper Brothers with Tommy Cannon and he fell about laughing and said could he have it and since then has used it in their act. Fred Smith was Chairman at the New Burley Club in Leeds and after I had done my act there one lunchtime, he very kindly invited me back to his house for a meal before I returned to the club for an evening performance. He introduced me to his charming wife Mary in their kitchen and I asked if I could use their toilet which was an outside loo at the bottom of their garden, The door of the toilet had gaps at the top and bottom and I was very embarrassed when Mary rattled the sneck on the door and asked, "How do you like your Yorkshire puddings, Norman?"At Thorne Moorends club, their concert secretary made me laugh once when, just before he announced me on stage, he picked up the microphone and asked, "Could gentlemen please refrain from peeing in the passageway. Last night the saddle on my bike was soaking wet." One concert secretary looking me up and down, said "Are you funny?" I said that I thought I was and he introduced me in a solemn voice, "The next act coming on is John Collier from Hull. He says he's funny so let's see how funny he really is." What a build up. At another club the resident band were tuning up in their dressing room when a committee man opened the door and told them in no uncertain terms to keep the noise down as members could not hear the bingo caller. "We're only warming up "said the trumpet player. "Warming up? Warming up? You've been the resident band here for six months, surely you know what to play by now. "came the reply. It was known that at a certain club on a Sunday lunchtime an old member would sit just near to the stage, reading a newspaper while the act was on. If he thought that the act was any good then he would put his newspaper down and listen. The audience would judge the act by his behaviour until one Sunday a certain comic who was having a hardtime, leant forward, took out his cigarette lighter and set fire to the guy's newspaper. I don't think the old man ever did it again. I was appearing at a club in Tredagar in Wales one lunchtime when a sheep wandered into the club. "Is he a member?" I quipped, "Has he been signed in as a guest?" Didn't raise many laughs from the club goers I'm afraid. Perhaps it was a regular occurrence! Little Alf was concert secretary at Wheatley Workingmen's Club in Doncaster. He had a favourite saying, "It gives me great pleasure", but he followed this up one night with "to announce the death of one of our respected members." Whoops! But he continued, "All rise please and show your appreciation, er, sorry your respect. Organist, please play something mournful." He then thanked everyone and moved straight into my introduction. I couldn't get going and tears of laughter streamed down my cheeks. At the Greaseborough club, between Rotherham and Sheffield, "Toes Piano Jacobson" played the piano with his feet and as an encore he shaved a volunteer from the audience with a cut-throat razor Now you don't get talent like that nowadays, do you?!! One act featured a 3ft Wallaby and the owner kept it on a lead until one day it broke free, jumped over a nearby wall and it hasn't been seen since! Gilbert and Son was a guy and his chimpanzee and it was a popular act in clubs for a few years.

I made my first television appearance in an ITV production 'Let's Laugh' in Didsbury and the show featured Johnny Hackett, Les Dawson, David Hamilton and Tom Jones and the Jones Boys and Tom arrived in a small, battered blue van. At that time there were lots of clubs in the Manchester area and showbiz people would meet up in the Chinatown area for an after-show meal, drinks and general chit-chat. Funny, I can never remember any of us admitting to having had a bad night on stage! Les Dawson and I became good friends and I was delighted when Les and his wife Meg asked me to be godfather to their daughter Pamela at her christening in Lytham St Annes.

In 1970, my manager, Harry Gunn told me about a phone call he had had from TV Producer Johnny Hamp who had devised a pilot programme which he was about to offer to Yorkshire Television. It was to be based on comics telling quickfire jokes direct to camera, one joke after another, in front of a live audience. Auditions were to be held in Manchester and Harry told me all the details of the proposed show. I was appearing in Bridlington at the time and I could not make it from the east coast and across the Pennines --- it was in the days before the M62 motorway was built and so I turned the offer down. Of course, the show became an immediate success on television and it became a 'must see' programme each week for millions of viewers, making stars of Charlie Williams, Bernard Manning, George Roper, Duggie Brown, Ken Goodwin, Frank Carson, Mick Miller, Stan Boardman and Mike Reid. Ah well, some you win and some you lose. I was shortly to come into contact with Johnny Hamp once again. In the 1950's I often met up with a guy called Ted Denyer who had an act involving playing a battered old trumpet, dressed in a railwayman's clothing and it was very funny to watch. Ted worked for the North Eastern Railway Company at Cannon Street Station near to where I then lived. We were chatting outside his office one afternoon when he said, " Well Norman, I must go as I've got some wheel tapping and shunting to do in the yard." I had no idea what he meant but he explained it was tapping wheels of the train coaches with a hammer to check their alignment was ok and shunting was driving a small engine and pushing several trains around in the marshalling area of the station yard (I think that's what he said!). The saying intrigued me and I built it into a Concert Chairman / Secretary act. Shortly after I had missed the audition for 'The Comedians' TV show, I was appearing at the 'Talk of the North' club in Eccles, Manchester and of course I included this in my act, as I had done for quite

47

some time. One night, Johnny Hamp, Bernard Manning and Colin Crompton came to see the show and I thought nothing more of it until I saw a new, late night programme on ITV called 'Wheeltappers and Shunters Social Club' which was produced by Johnny Hamp in Granada TV's studios in Manchester and it featured clubland acts with Bernard Manning compering the show and Colin Crompton acting as a concert secretary which was a take off of the act I had been doing for years. even using the name in my imaginary club, "The Wheeltappers and Shunters"; I did appear on the show in 1974 though.

7

Norman Collier

2009

I got the idea for my 'microphone breaking - up 'act from the Doncaster Wheatley workingmens club. I was at the side of the stage waiting to go on after the bingo had been called, in fact I was just one number off the jackpot! The club's PA system was faulty and every time the bingo caller shouted out a number, his voice broke up. It was hysterical and I had tears in my eyes as mayhem reigned throughout the club with members desperately trying to listen and mark their bingo cards correctly. When I looked down, I could see that the plug was loose in its socket and the caller also spotted this and shouted to his committee pal Charlie to give the damn plug a kick. I perfected this into my act and have used it regularly ever since. While we were on holiday in Miami with my wife Lucy and daughter Karen, we got friendly with an old lady in the hotel and she suggested going out together one evening to a nearby nightclub. It was only a small club with a compere called Frankie Seer and the old lady told him I was an entertainer from England and the next thing I heard was Frankie introducing me on stage. I insisted I was on holiday but he persisted and I made my way, somewhat reluctantly onto the stage and I took the microphone off him and went straight into my 'mic breaking up' act. Frankie looked at me agog. I said, "It's your guitar player." "No it ain't "he replied. "It must be your drummer then "was my reply." No, it ain't him either, he's not wired up "continued Frankie. He then proceeded to strip out the plug and checked out the socket and the mains switchboard, totally unaware that I was stringing him along until I owned up just before he rumbled me and he pretended to punch me on the chin before clapping me off the stage. At the end of a pleasant night I was approached by an agent called Andy Comargo and he asked me if I would like to work in Miami. I told him that I had plenty of work back home in England but he asked me to send him some data which I later did, enclosing my biography and some photographs but I didn't receive a reply from him. This rankled a bit with me so I decided to fly out again and see what was going on. My wife Lucy thought I was crazy but I had some time off so I went to the address on his business card which he had given me but he was no longer there so I went back to the nightclub where we had originally met and the manager there told me that Andy Comargo no longer booked their acts for them and he had no idea where he could be contacted.

The trip was a complete waste of time but I thought that while I was in America I would visit Las Vegas and I booked an internal flight. When I arrived I asked a cab driver to take me to the cheapest hotel he knew. He laughed and dropped me off at a motel opposite the Dunes Hotel and comedian Freddy Sales was on the bill, like me he was from Hull but we didn't really know each other that well. Ray Fell was on at The Flamingo and I had worked the Manchester clubs with him. Tom Jones was starring at Caesar's Palace and I had worked with Tom before and I was so excited that he was doing so well. After checking in at the motel, I had a bite to eat and then asked the receptionist if it was far to walk to Caesars Palace or would I have to get a cab as I was going to see Tom Jones who I knew from England. The hotel staff were very impressed and sent me off in the right direction, about a mile down the strip. When I arived I was not allowed to go to the cabaret room upstairs -- a burly, black cop with a gun in a holster made that abundantly clear to me despite my protestations. I hung around watching the action at the roulette tables when a waitress asked me if I would like a drink. She had a broad Midlands accent and she recognised me. I explained that I would like to meet up with my friend Tom, She agreed to take me through the kitchen area to the dressing rooms where Tom's son Mark took one look at me and started laughing. He was managing his dad's affairs and Tom came out of his dressing room, Californian tan and looking fabulous in an immaculate suit and Cuban heel shoes. He was checking his shirt cuffs and when he looked up and saw me, he burst out laughing and said "S*** Norman, That's all I need before going on stage". Mark aranged for us to have our photographs taken together and also very kindly fixed me up with a ticket to see the whole show which was tremendous. The audience were mainly women who screamed throughout, throwing their knickers on stage while Tom was singing. With me, they threw their corsets! There was plenty of champagne after the show and Tom and I had a lot to talk about our early days. He made me most welcome and it was a memorable night for me. When I eventually returned to the motel, the receptionist handed me the key and asked if I would like a woman in my room. Thinking of Lucy I replied 'I've enough with the one at home in England, thank you.' She muttered to herself "What a strange guy."

I suppose I have also become well-known for my chicken impressions. Some clubs and theatres even billed me as 'Norman Collier - The Chicken Man.' Even these days, I cannot go anywhere without someone clucking at me. Many's the time I've been having a meal in a restaurant and someone's walked by flapping their arms. Policemen in Hull have flagged me down in my car on the way home from an engagement and when they recognised me, they couldn't wait to cluck and squawk at me. One constable, after stopping me, shouted across to his mate who was trying to round up a couple of runaway horses under a nearby flyover. 'Hey, look who's here, it's the turkey - trot man.' The original skiffleman and one-time banjo player with Chris Barber's jazz. band, the great Lonnie Donegan started it all off. We were having a party backstage at the Globe Theatre in Stockton on Tees at the end of a successful week there and someone accidently knocked a plate of sandwiches off a table onto the floor and I got down on both knees and pretended to pick up the breadcrumbs with my mouth and moved my head backward and forward in a chicken - like motion. Lonnie doubled up with laughter and insisted I put the chicken impression into my act which I did and the thing has stuck with me ever since, even bringing me television advertisement jobs with the Kentucky Fried Chicken Company. I recorded two discs, 'Space Chicken' and 'The Singing Chicken' both written and produced by friend Bob Suntar and they sold thousands of copies (they are all still in boxes in my garage at home!). BBC Producer Barney Colehan insisted that I did my chicken impression on my first performance at the Leeds City Varieties and the chicken leg-end was born although little did I suspect that it would stay with me for so long. Rod Hull and his Emu were on the same bill that night and we did something together and I remember the blasted Emu grabbed me by the privates with its beak while we were on stage. Whenever I appeared on television, producers always insisted I did my chicken bit but I wasn't always happy to agree because I did not want people to think that was all I did. However, why should I complain as it became a sort of talisman for me

Another act from Hull, singer Ronnie Hilton, was also a good pal of mine over many years and together with David Whitfield, the three 'Hullites' would often meet up in each other's dressing rooms. He had four brothers and a sister and Ronnie went to Paisley Street School. What a lovely voice he had. We both appeared in 'The Happiness Show' at the Arcadia

Theatre in Skegness in the summer of 1965. We were passing the time of day in the town centre one afternoon when we came across a little lad of about four or five who was crying and said he had lost his mam and dad in the nearby amusement arcade. I was comforting him but Ronnie saw an opportunity for him and the show we were both in and he told me to ring the local newspaper which I did and they sent a photographer straight away and the headline to a large photograph of Ronnie and the little boy appeared in the next day's paper as 'Singing star finds lost boy' with a report. The boy's parents had actually came out of the amusement arcade after five minutes or so but what an eye Ronnie had for photo-opportunity!.

8

Norman Collier

2009

I was appearing in a nationwide tour in the Black and White Minstrel Show in Bristol in the autumn of 1971 when my agent received an invitation from impresario Bernard Delfont to appear in the Royal Command Variety Performance at the London Palladium on November 15th. I ended up £100 out of pocket, a lot of money in those days, as I had to pay comic Derek Dene to stand in for me in Bristol as part of my contract and of course artistes never charged a fee to appear in a Royal Command Performance as it was such an honour to be invited, Before the rehearsal drill, I went down to Tommy Cooper's dressing room to introduce myself. He was a great favourite of mine but we had never actually met, I knocked on his door and poked my head round. Tommy was sat there in his long johns, his trademark red fez on his head and a glass of something in his hand. He had a few friends with him so I said, "Hello Tommy, Norman Collier. I just wanted to introduce myself." Tommy stood up and shook my hand. "Hello Norman. Nice to meet you. He's not got a drink. Have you got a drink Norman?. "I laughed and politely refused." What are you laughing at?" he said, a bit abruptly. "Nothing Tommy, I just wanted to meet you, that's all" I replied and after wishing him well, I closed his dressing room door and went down the corridor and back to my own dressing room.

Over the years, I have always regretted having no photographs of one of the greatest nights of my career. Thirty five years later I got a telephone call from Granada Television who were filming a series of interviews with artistes who had appeared in Royal Command Performances since 1960 and they intended linking the interviews with actual performance highlights for a five part series on ITV3. My old pal Bernie Clifton had given my details to the programme researchers and I went down to London by Hull Trains to film an interview. During a break in the filming I mentioned to the interviewer my regret at not having a recording of the evening and they very kindly ran off a copy of my act on the night. I watched it at home the next day with my family and I never realised that I had actually had a conversation with Her Majesty Queen Elizabeth at the after - show introductions and I have absolutely no idea what we talked about. Fancy me forgetting that!!

1971 was quite a year for me as I won the Supreme Award in a BBC TV contest for club land artistes and I also won the comedy section on ITV's 'Ace of Clubs' programme. I became the first comic to make three consecutive appearances on David Nixon's BBC TV show 'Comedy Bandbox' which was followed by appearances on BBC TV's 'The Good Old Days' and ITV's 'Let's Laugh' and 'Clubnight' productions. I bought myself a new BMW 2500 car in bright orange and drove it the forty miles from home to Scarborough where I was booked to appear at the Futurist Theatre along with the Bachelors singing group and impressionist Mike Yarwood. Mike wasn't very well at the time and was clearly lacking in self - confidence, He was very self -critical and admitted to me that he very rarely watched his television programmes.

With all this national recognition, I suppose it was natural to be invited to join the Grand Order of Water Rats which is a charitable organisation of variety performers. In the summer of 1889, a comedian called Joe Elvin bought a small trotting pony and named it 'Magpie'. Within a few weeks Joe had got a small syndicate together and 'Magpie' began winning races around the London area. The group used the winnings to help performers who had hit hard times and they were also among the first to instigate soup kitchens in London's east end for the poor and refugees ariving from Eastern Europe. One day they were taking 'Magpie' back to the stables in the pouring rain and the driver of a horse-drawn London bus saw them and shouted, "Blimey, what you got there? Looks like a blooming water rat." The group took the comment on board and founded the Grand Order of Water Rats. Current membership is 180.

9

Norman Collier

2009

I had a lot of fun on charity golf days, especially on Jimmy Tarbuck's tournaments in Spain and we provided quite a few 'Sunshine Coaches' for kids as members of the Variety Club of Great Britain. I was overwhelmed with support from celebrities for my own charity golf days, with locals Keith Dearnley and Richard Stead organising things for me and local businesses also gave me some grand support. It was wonderful to mix with so many stars at the various golf tournaments - Eric Sykes, Fred Trueman, Bobby Charlton, Johnny Mathis, Robert Powell, Vince Miller, Phil Middlemiss, Stan Boardman, DennisTaylor, John H Stacey, Henry Cooper, Tony Curie, Jasper Carott, Ian Mercer, Russ Abbot, Rick Wakeman, Les Dennis, Tommy Cannon, Frank Carson, Eddie Large, Trevor Bannister, Mike England, Nobby Stiles, Howard Kendall, big Ron Atkinson, Willie Morgan, Rodney Marsh and Willie John McBride among them, A charity golf day held in my name for Duncan Walker of the Leeds Hospital for Children was held at Hull Golf Club and raised £20,000 with support from Bobby Charlton, Charlie Williams, Roy Walker, Shakin' Stevens, Tony Barton, Roger De Courcey, Dennis Taylor, Ronato, Cliff Thorburn and Tommy Cannon.

The game of golf was the cause of two of the most hurtful incidents I have ever experienced, albeit indirectly. I was playing a round with a couple of friends at the Springhead Golf Club, a municipal course on the outskirts of Hull and I was looking for my ball in a shallow ditch when a stray ball from an adjoining fairway hit me so hard on the calf that the letters 'cle' of the Pinnacle ball were imprinted on my skin. There was blood everywhere but luckily for me it had happened near to the car park and my partners took me to my own doctor, Bob Blair, at his surgery and he had a look, packed ice round it and sent me off to the A and E Dept at Hull Royal Infirmary for an x-ray. A Belgian doctor looked at my injury "Oh dear. Not good. If you play football, you not play for a long time" he said. A Geordie male nurse then iced my leg and I was wheeled through to the x-ray dept in a wheel-chair before being discharged and my golfing partners took me home to Welton. But back to my golf incident. When I walked in at home, I don't remember getting much sympathy from Lucy.

Some weeks later, the swelling on my leg had gone down and I could walk without limping. I received a phone call one afternoon, "Hello Mr Collier. Doctor Barnado's Home," the voice at the other end of the phone said. "Oh, I didn't know the Doctor had been away "I replied and that failed to raise a laugh. During the course of the conversation it transpired that the charity had heard about my charitable efforts in the past and were looking for some help in fund-raising. They wanted me to appear at Robert Fossett's Circus at the Walton Street Fairground site the next week and let the elephant Dum Dum walk over me as I laid in the circus ring as a stunt and then Dr Barnado's helpers would collect money from the audience. Of course, I agreed to help and duly presented myself at the circus tent at the appointed hour and the elephant's lady trainer rehearsed me in the Big Top. "Now then Mr Collier, you just lay down on this mat and when I tap you on the shoulder with my cane, you please roll over to your left. Do not roll over to the right as Dum Dum would crush you" she said which wasn't very re-assuring. The time came for the actual performance which was an afternoon matinee and there weren't many people there. I laid down on the mat to the sound of trumpet fanfare backing tapes and the lady ringmaster, resplendent in her red jacket and cream breeches, gave me a great build - up. The elephant lumbered across and stepped over me just as we had rehearsed that morning, The smell of its stomach was awful and the feeling terrible as it brushed its trunk across my face but it was over quickly. A charming lady came to thank me but she had only collected nine pence in her white enamel bucket. All that for just nine pence! Dum Dum's trainer then came across to me and asked if I would mind posing for a photograph with the two of them outside of the circus tent. A photographer from the Hull Daily Mail took his pictures and then a news agency snapper came across. As he took a picture, Dum Dum stepped back, perhaps startled by the flash gun and promptly caught me on the same leg as the one which had suffered the golf ball injury. The elephant's leg took a big piece of skin off my leg and once more my blood was everywhere. I called for the trainer to take me to her caravan nearby and asked for some ice to be put on my injury. She didn't speak much English and produced a pack of frozen peas from her fridge which helped. They called an ambulance for me and the nurses at Hull Royal Infirmary A and E patched me up with instructions to let my own doctor have a look and change the dressing on the wound the next morning. I went to the surgery and Dr Blair came through to see me sitting in his waiting room with my leg up on a chair. "Hello Norman" he smiled"Not another golf ball accident?" "No Doctor, an elephant kicked me on the shin yesterday" I replied. With that comment from me, he burst out laughing, "Oh Norman, you're such a funny man." That was no real consolation to me as I was still in considerable pain. I was going to tell him about two circus clowns leading a camel past me as I was being helped into the trainer's caravan the previous afternoon and it had spat at me but I decided against sharing the experience with him as it would have added insult to injury.

10

Norman Collier

2009

Pantomime was something I always enjoyed and looked forward to, probably because I was just a big kid myself. I was usually cast as Widow Twanky or the Wicked Baron but I certainly didn't object to being type cast. One Christmas I pulled a muscle behind my right knee (Hypochondriac? Me??). I had jumped down the last two steps of the theatre stairs and cockled on my ankle when I landed. It was yet another visit to a hospital where I was bandaged up and sent away with a loaned pair of crutches. I was in a bit of pain but I was determined not to miss the evening performance and I limped on stage with the crutches, right on cue, and confided to the audience with a big wink, "I thought I was booked to play Baron Hard Up, not Long John Silver", and that brought the house down.

When I was in panto in Liverpool, I often visited Jimmy McGreogan, the Everton FC physiotherapist, for a bit of lamp treatment and a massage. I was on his treatment table one afternoon at Goodison Park when in walked Bill Shankly, the Liverpool FC manager, who evidently was a regular visitor. "Hello laddie" he said to me in his gruff Scottish accent, "How are you? I've just been to a funeral and you would have thought it'd been a better day than this, wouldn't you? Bloody rain." I was playing Baron Hard Up once again, this time at the Palace Theatre in Manchester, in 1987. Michael Barrymore was the star and Jessica Martin played Cinderella. I also appeared with Michael at the Bournemouth International Centre with Lulu and Liverpool comic Hal Nolan the next year. The first night of summer shows was always full of the resort's landladies who were invited along as 'freebies' so that they could 'spread the word' among their summertime guests on how good (hopefully !) the show was. Michael came on stage, stood on his head and cajoled the audience, "Enjoy yourselves, ladies, they can't hang you for it." He was certainly an unusual character. I had a great time in Cinderella at the Tameside Theatre in Ashton under Lyne in 1990 with Chris Quintin (Coronation Street's Brian Tilsley), Foo Foo Lammar and Umberto as the Ugly Sisters, Jeanette Richmond as Cinderella, Paul Hendy played Buttons, Ann Duval was the Fairy Godmother and my son Vic played the Brokers Man, Jess Conrad was a great Prince Charming and we all had a real ball over the forty seven performances. Tom Mennard was another good friend of mine and we appeared together in 'Goody Two Shoes' at Hull New Theatre in 1969 along with Sandy Lane, Jimmy Thompson and McDonald Hobley. A big advantage was that I could get home every night after the show but it was always a strange experience for me whenever I appeared at the 'New' as it was only about 150 yards away from where I was born.

After seven years under Harry Gunn's management, I decided it was time for a change of agency and I moved to Phil and Dorothy Solomon's agency in London but I decided to remain living in East Yorkshire although I hated staying in lodgings or 'digs'. There was usually a list of recommended premises on the stage door notice board at most theatres. Every landlady seemed to have a cat, budgie or parrot and an aspidistra in the front room and when you called on a Sunday night, suitcase in hand, an upstairs window would be thrown open after you had knocked on the front door. "What do you want?" "I'd like to stay here, please." "Well, stay there then." The window would be slammed shut. You would have thought that she would have put a 'No Vacancies' sign in the window, wouldn't you?! You could always tell when suet pudding was on the evening menu when the landlady came through from the kitchen wearing only one stocking. Room charges then were around £10 a week with three meals a day usually included. I once shared a room with Emile Ford ('What do you want to make those eyes at me for?') in Manchester and we were served sponge cakes in rich onion gravy as a main course one evening. The landlady, bless her, had thought they were Yorkshire puddings and she blamed her poor eyesight when we pointed out her mistake. Dot Ackroyd was a real character. She ran lodgings in Cheetham Hill in Manchester. "No need to set your alarm tomorrow morning Norman, you'll hear me scraping the toast" she joked. Dot was a lovely lady and another nice person was Helen Bradley. Her lodgings were very luxurious - piano in the lounge, chandeliers in the dining room, napkins at the table. She once confided in me about an outrageous comedian; "He'll not stay here again, Norman. He peed on my little dog.' I did hear of one landlady who asked her guests not to put the chamber pot back under the bed if they used it during the night as the "the steam rusts the bed springs."

My wife Lucy liked to travel with me during the summer months when the kids were on school holidays. She persuaded me to buy a touring caravan to tow behind our Volvo car. I travelled across the Pennines to Manchester to buy a 15ft ABI caravan from Ken O'Neil and I towed it down to Norfolk when I was booked to appear in a summer season at Great Yarmouth in the Little and Large Show. We booked to stay on a caravan site in nearby Caister. Now I am not proud of the fact but I am totally hopeless with anything remotely mechanical and after unhitching the caravan on arrival, I had absolutely no idea how to stabilise the damned thing. I suppose one of the benefits of fame is being recognised and straight away four burly chaps came to our rescue. "Now then Norman. Stand over there and leave it to us" said the tattooed one and I was more than happy to do as I was told and the lads soon had everything organised. It certainly saved me a lot of pulling and panting (and cursing !) but there was a downside. My theatre season lasted for sixteen weeks, ninety nine consecutive performances, playing to packed houses every day with Little and Large topping the bill and Frank Carson and Rodger Stevenson's Puppets also starred. Word soon got round the site and youngsters would knock on the caravan door at all times of the day and ask for my autograph or requesting I do my chicken impression for them. I never refused but we did want some privacy and a little bit of time to ourselves.

We spent a lot of time with all the theatre performers that summer and what lovely people they all were. – Syd, Eddie, Frank and their wives. When we got back home from the theatre it was usually well past midnight and I always liked to have a good wash in the caravan site's communal washroom before I went to bed. I had notes pushed under the toilet door asking for my autograph and one time I was brushing my teeth when I became aware of a guy at the next wash basin giving me the stare. "Don't I know you? Do you work for Thorne Electrics? "he asked." No, not me pal," I replied but he wouldn't give up. "I've got it. You're that comedian who's appearing on the pier show in Great Yarmouth. John Collier, isn't it? No, No, I'm wrong. Norman Collier. That's it. We've been to see the show twice this week, Great." He then called out to someone in the nearby cubicle. "Hey Herbert, you'll never guess who I'm talking to out here.It's Norman Collier." "Well blow me down" chortled Herbert as he flushed the toilet and came out of the cubicle, grabbing my hand in a firm handshake. Now I am very particular about personal cleanliness, washing hands etc, and I quickly gathered up my towel, soap and bag and dashed off, muttering my excuses. I ran back to our caravan and washed my hands thoroughly under the little geyser. Lucy was sat up in bed reading and

Dum Dum the elephant steps over me at Robert Fossett's Circus in Hull as part of a charity stunt which eventually backfired on me

My son Vic married Margaret Dunn at St Nicholas Church in Beverley. June 1973

"Hurry up dad, we're late" My daughter Karen's marriage to John Ainsley in Welton Village. June 1979

My daughter Janet on her wedding day

Chick, Chick, Chick, Chick Chicken ...... I was always requested to include my chicken
routine in my act, especially in pantomimes.

Five generations of my family in August 1991. My mother Mary, myself, my daughter Janet, grand-daughter Rebekah and great-grand-daughter Lois.

My son Victor (left) enjoying a joke with comic Bobby Ball and myself

Roy Walker with myself at singer Tony Dalli's restaurant in Marbella after a charity golf tournament in Spain with boxer Henry Cooper, Manchester United manager Sir Matt Busby, Manchester United and England footballer Bobby Charlton and his wife Norma. Bobby was knighted in 1994 and Henry in 2000

Snooker stars Cliff Thorburn abd Dennis Taylor help the search for some sunshine at my charity golf day at the Hull Golf Club in April 1987.

Peter Alliss seeking my advice, again, on how to improve his golf game!

Bobby Charlton, Charlie Williams, Shakin' Stevens, Tony Barton, Russ Abbot, Eddie Large and Paul Shane kindly supported my golf tournament at the Hull Golf Club in April 1987

Lucy and me with Howard Keel. I was always delighted to be invited to compete in the Howard Keel Golf Classics Tournaments.

My wife Lucy, myself and organisers Keith Dearnley and Richard Stead present Duncan Walker of Killinbeck Children's Hospital in Leeds with a cheque for £17,000 part of the money raised at my charity golf day held at the Hull Golf Club in April 1987.

Sir Cliff Richard kindly invited my wife Lucy and I backstage at the Edinburgh Playhouse in November 1996 when he was touring in the musical 'Heathcliff'

My wife Lucy eyes up the sausage roll I was trying to feed comedy actor Norman Wisdom with at his home on the Isle of Man.

"Woodman, woodman, spare that tree." I was pleased to be asked to support the "I'm with Woody" campaign in September 1991.

What's this? A chicken pulling comedians Syd Little and Eddie Large in a rickshaw? We all had some good fun in the panto Aladdin at Hull New Theatre in 1986.

I also had a lot of laughs appearing with Russ Abbot on his London Weekend TV show "Madhouse"

Ventriloquist Neville King and I share the same zany humour.

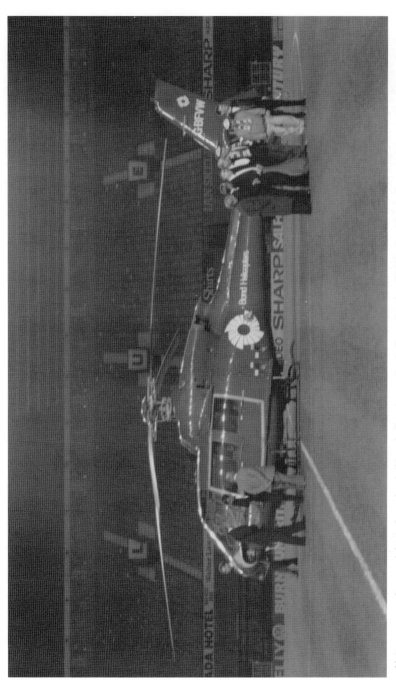

Not many people can claim to have landed in a helicopter on the hallowed turf at Old Trafford football ground. I was appearing with Roy Walker in a summer season at Blackpool's North Pier and we were flown from Blackpool Airport for a charity function in Manchester United's corporate entertainment suite. Roy and I are on the right, both wearing Man Utd scarves.

I spent a delightful lunch chatting to legendary comic Eric Sykes at the Hull Quality Royal Hotel in November 2005.

Four good pals of mine --- Paul Adams, Duncan Norvelle, Frank Carson and Jimmy Cricket

asked me what on earth I was doing and had I cut myself or something. I said that I had just shook hands with a guy. "You're eccentric, you are" she said and carried on reading! I much preferred renting a house or flat for a summer season but it was expensive, not so bad when I could afford it but I think back to the days when five of us from the same show shared one bedroom in lodgings in Sunderland and the other four kept me awake all night with their loud snoring. Although it was expensive it was great for Lucy and me to take the kids with us in the summer months. In 1969 I paid £300 to rent a house for a week in Bournemouth when Frankie Vaughan and Mike Yarwood topped the bill.

Very often during the summer season artistes were often asked to open local fetes or attend charity garden parties. Terry Hall, the ventroliquist, had Lenny the Lion character dummy and at one such event, the local vicar, who was also Chairman of the village organising committee, came up to Terry and said, "Excuse me, Mr Hall, but time is marching on. How long will it take you to get into your skin costume?" Such is fame. Terry also told me of an incident when he had lost his voice due to a throat infection and the theatre manager rang a local doctor for him. "Could you come and see Lenny the Lion and give him something for his throat infection?" "You don't need me, you need a vet" was the doctor's reply. If I was away from home for very long, it was difficult to avoid becoming bored during the day-time and before an evening performance. I liked playing golf and usually joined up with the guys from the show and played by invitation at a local golf club or sometimes I would drive out into the surrounding countryside and just sit in the car and admire the scenery. If there was a film I particularly wanted to see, I would take myself off to the nearest cinema. I like horseracing and if there was a meeting at a nearby racecourse then I would head off there. I once owned a share in a racehorse but I owned the back half and it always came in second and it once finished a race so late that the jockey was wearing his pyjamas. Frankie Vaughan, Peter Goodright and me once appeared on the same show at the Congress Theatre in Eastbourne and on the Wednesday afternoon, Frankie invited me to join him at Lewes racecourse and he offered to pick me up at the theatre in his beautiful wine coloured Rolls Royce Corniche and we looked forward to a good afternoon's racing. Frankie knew some trainers at the meeting and after talking to one of them, he came back and whispered to me out of the corner of his mouth, "I've had a good tip for the third race, horse called Channel Eleven and I suggest we both back it to win." I put £65 on the nag but it came in third and a long way off the front. It was a lot of money for me to lose then but I consoled myself that Frankie had also lost money. "That was a great tip, Frankie. How much did you put on the damned horse?" I asked and I was speechless when he told me he had only put on a 5/- each way bet.

There were some wonderful character acts in my variety theatre days. Chain smoking Jimmy James and Eli Wood and Jimmy once told me, "Norman, quickest spot we ever did was one Friday night at the Glasgow Empire. 500 Scots willing us to try and make them laugh and we failed miserably.' Eli confided in me, "I'm good with hecklers Norman, if they'll wait" as he had a pronounced stage stutter. Roy Castle later joined them as their stooge and what a wonderful trio they were. Murray Smith, top hat and tails, came on stage smoking and pretending to be drunk, although some of the time he was not pretending. Roger and Veronica Mistin had a roller-skating act on stage. 'Sit well back' advised the compere to those in the front rows. What about the tightrope walker, who would murmur, "You can come out here some nights and never see a soul." No idea what he meant.

During a week's work touring clubs in the North East, I had been racked with pain every night with a pulled muscle in my neck and on the last evening, a Saturday, I was due to at The Sands in Whitley Bay but the acute pain turned to agony I just could not go on and decided to go home I had a Daimler Sovereign automatic and I was driving back down the A1 in excrutiating pain when I saw a bloke thumbing a lift. I thought I'll pick him up, at least it will be a bit of company. I stopped and as he opened the passenger door he could see the pained look on my face. "Do you want me to drive?" he said Some relief at last I thought and I staggered round the back of the car to swop places with him. I could now see he was drunk and as he sat in the driver's seat he asked me where the gear stick was. What the hell was I doing with a drunken bloke I had never met before, driving an automatic car he had never driven before?! We muddled through somehow and he got out at Yarm and I managed to drive the rest of the way home to Welton. I saw Doctor Bob Blair the next morning and he got me into Hull Royal Infirmary straight away where I was put into traction for ten days with a diagnosis of a slipped disc in my back. I could only drink tea through the spout of the teapot and I had to eat food from a tray strapped across my chest. I woke up one morning to see a bearded gentleman with thick-lens glasses looking down at me. I thought it was a Catholic priest giving me the last rites but it turned out he was from the local Seaman's Mission.

Frankie Vaughan was appearing at the Westfield Country Club in Cottingham that week and he came to visit me in hospital. He came down the ward laughing like mad and then everyone started laughing. "What have you been doing, Norman?" were his first words to me and one of the nurses called out to Frankie, "Roses grow on you "which prompted him to respond, "That's NORMAN Vaughan, nurse. Not me." (Norman was regularly advertising Roses chocolates on ITV at the time). I was discharged from hospital with the instruction to wear a neck brace for the next six weeks but I was booked to appear at the Cresta Club in Birmingham in two weeks time and I didn't want to cancel a second engagement (the show must go on, you know!!) and a good friend recommended me to see a Mr Stowe who was a bone setter in the Boulevard in Hull. I made an appointment with him and his first words to me were "Take off the neck brace, please" which I did. "What do you do for a living" he asked. "Comedy, I think "I replied, He gently straightened me up and put me in an arm lock around my neck and something clicked and I felt a sharp pain for a few seconds but then instant relief. I gingerly moved my neck from side to side. Wonderful. No pain at all. "Thank you, Mr Stowe. How much do I owe you ?" "Give me 5/- and tell Hull Royal Infirmary you sneezed and the pain went" he said.

I'm not much of a cricket fan but I was once booked for a dinner in the Long Room at Lord's Cricket Ground. There must have been 200 MCC gentlemen present and I was asked to perform from a rostrum. I felt like a priest giving a sermon. Normally I need a table of some sort to keep my props bag on. Glass doors from the Long Room lead out onto the steps down to the pitch and I started off by opening the doors, peered out into the black night and turned back to the guests with the comment, "I see Boycott's still batting then." I thought it was quite a good gag but the response was absolutely nil so that was a disappointing start to an entirely forgettable night for me in London NW8. I get a brief mention in Bill Frindall's book 'Bearders - My Life in Cricket' with a tale of Leslie Crowther giving a speech in Basingstoke and the battery-operated microphone malfunctioned and Bill wrote "Norman Collier built an entire act around a malfunctioning microphone but Leslie experienced a real life experience."

11

Norman Collier

2009

I have made quite a few television advertisements, promoting various products. Kentucky Fried Chicken was an obvious subject for me, bearing in mind my chicken act. I was booked to film a tv ad for them and duly turned up at the London studios and a young lady from the advertising agency met me at reception and asked, "Where's your chicken costume, Mr Collier?" I politely informed her that I didn't have a costume and that I used the jacket sleeves of my suit to start off my chicken impression. This certainly seemed to surprise her. They made me a special jacket and a stuntman showed me how they would set fire to the jacket sleeves and I would dash across the room, flapping my arms and shouting, "Where's my hot wings, where's my hot wings?", would then be drenched with buckets of cold water thrown over me and I would then walk slowly back across the room, thoroughly drenched and muttering dark thoughts. It took three takes to complete before the Commercial Director was happy and he asked the crew to give me a round of applause, which they did and I trotted off to get dried. I was a ventriloquist's dummy, advertising cookers in a British Gas TV ad and lately I have done some commercials for motorised wheelchairs. A television Summertime Special in a marquee in Eastbourne, when Shirley Bassey topped the bill, is a vivid memory. The programme producer asked me what I was going to do. I said I wanted a car door with a wind-down window and I worked out a sketch where I would be the car driver and wind down the window to ask a passer-by the way to Beachy Head to be told to drive straight on whereupon I would stand up and walk off-stage with the car door. The producer's reply to my idea was, "I think the sun has got to you, Norman." In any case, the thing was vetoed because the door and glass were far too heavy to carry any distance. Later at home in Welton, I recounted the experience to my son Vic, who suggested we make a plywood door with a perspex window, which we did and I have performed the sketch many times with these improvised props. In 1987, Eric Sykes wrote and directed a thirty minute silent film, MR H IS LATE and he invited me to play a small part in it which involved me playing a blind pianist being hoisted up a multi - storey flat in a window cleaner's platform hoist. Now, I have no head for heights but Eric told me not to worry, just don't look down. In the end, I had no problem at all with the scene and when you look at the cast list, it's obvious why we had a lot of fun filming as it involved Eric, Jimmy Edwards, Spike Milligan, Mike Yarwood, Charlie Drake, Kathy Staff, Bob Todd, Henry McGee, Gabrielle Drake, Cannon and Ball, Richard O'Sullivan, Rula Lenska, Eli Wood, Dennis Waterman, Freddie Starr, Terry Scott, Peter Butterworth, Roy Kinnear, Paul Shane, John Alderton and Sylvia Sims. Twenty three characters who made me feel so at ease and gave me plenty of laughs.

I met up again with Eric Sykes at a Hull and East Yorkshire Literary Lunch in November 2005, when he was promoting his autobiography IF I DON'T WRITE IT, NOBODY ELSE WILL and he came up to Hull by train with his manager Norma Farnes. Neither of them knew I would be a guest at the lunch and it was nice to surprise them both at the pre-lunch reception. During his speech, Eric paid me the compliment of calling me ' the comedian's comedian' and the two of us as the 'last of the vaudevillians in this country' and we spent most of the lunch chatting about old times. We met up again in April 2006 in Willerby when Eric came back up to the area to promote the paperback edition of his autobiography and he very kindly offered to write a foreword for my book. In my estimation, I have the greatest of respect for Eric as a man and for his work. He has a rare and brilliant comedy mind and I am very proud to call him a friend.

I always enjoyed playing Leed City Varieties theatre, especially when my son Vic appeared with me, playing the accordion. My first - ever show there still embarrasses me when I think about it. I had done a ten minute spot before a packed house and having taken a bow, I made my way off just as the next act to appear, 'Franklyn and his doves', came on from the left. I had my props bag in my hand and went to exit right, pulling the red velvet curtain at the side of the stage back and expecting to see an exit door there but there was only a brick wall. Panic set in as the audience roared with laughter, no doubt thinking that it was all part of the act. Franklyn had his back to me and he was totally unaware of my continuing presence on stage as he puffed away on a cigarette in a silver holder, pulling white doves out of the most unlikely places with his immaculate white gloves. He must have thought that his act was getting its best - ever reception, such was the applause and laughter throughout the theatre. He eventually saw me out of the corner of his eye as I tried to shuffle off at the back of the stage and Franklyn sidled up to me and whispered, "Piss off, Collier." I eventually got off stage after what seemed like an eternity to me and I apologised profusely to Franklyn later in his dressing room. I certainly never made the same mistake again at that theatre. My son Vic picked up playing instruments without any formal training and we bought him a secondhand accordion which he taught himself to play at the age of 12. My daughter Janet sang, accompanied by Vic, at the Westminster Club in Doncaster when I was also on the bill and afterwards the club steward, Billy Carmichael, came across to see me at the end of the night and I got out my booking diary in anticipation of a re-book but he didn't want me, he wanted to book Janet and Vic again! Vic was once asked, "Are you related to Norman Collier?" "I've never heard of him" he replied but later on in the evening he did admit that he was my son but nobody believed him then. I was delighted when Vic and I appeared on the same bill at Leeds City Varieties Old Tyme Music Hall, made world famous through BBC TV's 'Good Old Days' programmes when around 600 people would dress up in Edwardian costumes to watch music hall acts introduced by an impressive Master of Ceremonies. My other daughter, Karen, once appeared with Vic and Janet at Hull Parks Open Air Theatre as a trio and accompanied by our dog!! Vic worked at Hawker Siddeley (aircraft) in Brough and later at British Rail and he now entertains at old folks homes (well, his audiences can't get up and leave the building, can they?!). He has also appeared with Max Bygraves' son in Paignton. I've been very honoured to be chosen to entertain our troops overseas many times. In Belfast, our coach was escorted from the airport to the barracks by armoured personnel carrier vehicles. I was appearing with vocalist Kim Cordell and as I did my act, I became aware of one soldier sitting in the front row with an Alsatian dog fast asleep. The dog had slept all through the night alongside its handler but I was just into my chicken routine when I saw the dog open one eye and let out a loud growl, open its other eye and with a much louder growl, tried to get to me on the improvised stage and it pulled its handler off his chair. I think it was the fastest stage exit ever made in my career, to be followed on stage by a wide-eyed Alan Randall, ready to perform his George Formby impersonation act with his ukelele in his hand but not exactly sure what was going on. Another time, I flew out to Newfoundland from Brize Norton RAF camp to entertain British troops there and then onto Belize in British Honduras, then to Gander and back to Brize Norton. I went through so many time zones, I came back younger than when I had set off. It was all very worthwhile just to shake hands with our lads abroad. I really did enjoy the Combined Services Entertainment bookings with compere Gordon Peters and we travelled to Limassol in Cyprus, British Honduras and Gaan. Ivor Emmanuel and I shared a few trips and we did meet up with ex-Major Derek Agutter, father of actress Jenny who became famous for her part in that excellent film 'The Railway Children'. Other artistes I met on these tours were Joe Brown, Wally Whyton and Julie Rogers while singer Matt Munro topped the bill at one show in Germany and what a nice sense of humour he had. After a show for the Dragoon Guards, we were all invited back to the Officer's Mess for food and drink and an officer said to me, in a plummy voice, "Norman, I loved your turkey trot. You must spend hours at the zoo, observing." I moved away quickly!

Comedian Tom Mennard was as daft as me. We were sitting next to each other on the plane home from one of these Forces shows and I think to relieve the boredom, he leaned across and started gently slapping my face --- "No more drink for you Collier." I caught on straight away and pretended to start shivering and I covered myself with a blanket, muttering again and again," Want some, want some." Two soldiers sat across the aisle had a bottle of whiskey on their seat fold-a-way tray and they put a newspaper over it to hide it from my sight. Eventually, a stewardess came and told Tom and I that if I was really ill, she would summon first aid for me but if not, would we please stop messing about. I would have had to keep up the pretence for the rest of the five hour flight so sleep was a better option!! On another trip back from Cyprus, I went to the toilet and whitened my face and watered my eyes to make myself look ill and then staggered down the aisle. An officer in civvies with a rolled up macintosh on his knees, looked me up and down with disdain. "I don't think you are very funny at all" he said, Just then there was some turbulance and I pretended to be ill all over him. So now I had to keep this ill act up and by the time we got back to Brize Norton, I really was ill. Served me right! Mike Harding, 'The Rochdale Cowboy', and myself appeared in Cyprus again for the troops for another CSE tour and Mike has a fabulous sense of humour. We both made each othe laugh although one night we got into some real trouble. I had gone to Mike's room for a drink after the gig and he was sat with a pig mask on and after a few drinks he decided he didn't like the table lamp so he threw it out the window then I decided I didn't like the stand, that went out as well until virtually everthing in the room had been thrown out of the window. We both thought it was hilarious. Sober and very embarrassed the next morning, we paid for the damage and promised not to do it again --- and we never have! I was booked for three shows in five days in Limassol on another occasion and halfway through my act on day one, 'Jimmy the Cypriot', a zany theatre impresario from the island, threw a live chicken on stage which certainly caused some pandemonium. The next day it was a piglet, more pandemonium spread through the room and the thing p***** on stage. I couldn't continue for laughing and Jimmy smiled and said, "tomorrow Norman, I bring a donkey with me" and it took all my might to persuade him otherwise. Most of the artistes on the tour spent the daytime topping up their tans on the beach or by the hotel pool but that bored me stiff and it was one of the reasons I took up the game of golf. I bought some clubs and enjoyed partnering Mike Reid in a pro am at the Belfry immediately before the British Open was played there and I eventually got my handicap down to 20.

The ventriloquist Neville King and I shared the same sense of humour. If you remember, his act involved an old man dummy, grey hair, flat cap and a red scarf wrapped round the neck. Neville once dressed his old man dummy in a khaki jacket and camouflage cap and he asked me to introduce him to Lord Mountbatten after a charity show we had both been involved in. I duly obliged and the dummy looked at him and said, "and where were you when it was all going on?" Lord Louis politely sniggered and carried on down the line meeting the rest of the company. When Nev and I were both appearing in the Black and White Minstrel Show in Bristol, we called in the nearby Horse and Jockey pub after a matinee show. There was no one in the pub lounge except the barman who was polishing glasses behind the bar. We both had a half of lager and it went down so well that I asked Neville if he fancied another half, which he did, so I went back up to the bar and ordered two more halves of lager and " two pickled, squawk, squawk, eggs please barman." Now I didn't mean anything offensive but the barman refused to serve me. I repeated the order with more squawks and a pecking action. I very rarely did my chicken act off stage but the barman stared me out and said icily, "Not in here,sir. Please get out." We realised he was being serious so we thought we had better leave but back at the theatre, we hatched a 'get our own back' plan for the next afternoon. Now, most entertainers keep a set of golf clubs in their carboots, just to pass the time away between shows by playing a round or two of golf at a local golf course but Nev was a keen shooter and rarely missed a chance to ask a local landowner for permission to shoot game on his land when he was on tour. The plan was for him to dress up in his full gear, long leather coat, knee length boots, shell belt and long barrelled gun --- and I wore a ginger beard, a large stetson hat and carried a battered old silver bugle. What must we have looked like?!! Anyway, the next afternoon, we went back to the pub, pushed open the door into the lounge where once again the barman was polishing glasses at the bar and I'll never forget the startled look on his face as I blew on the bugle, pulled my beard down and shouted, "two pickled eggs". As quick as we had entered the lounge, we scarpered back to the sanctuary of our dressing room in the theatre, laughing like two naughty schoolboys. Nev and I were booked to appear together at the O'Keefe Centre Theatre in Toronto, Canada in the show 'London Calling' with the versatile Des O'Connor topping the bill and it co-starred Dorothy Wayne. We all flew out together from Manchester and on arrival, we booked into a city centre hotel. A receptionist with a dead pan face awaited us. Alongside the reception desk was a large table with various tourist information and souvenirs on it, including some Canadian Mounties dolls. I picked one up and pretended to wind it up and sang, "When I'm calling you" very softly. Nev picked up a Red Indian doll from the same table and threw his voice, singing the same song but at a higher level. I then said to the receptionist, "Wrap these two dolls up for me will you love." She looked astonished. "Do you know, all the time I have worked in this hotel, I never knew they were singing dolls." The next morning we were both in the hotel gents for a wash and brush up and there was a chrome air purifier fixed above the washroom mirrors and it looked very much like an old-style microphone. Two elderly Canadian gentlemen came into the washroom and Nev pretended to talk into the purifier as though it was a two-way microphone. "I'd like to order breakfast for room 219 please. Sausages, bacon, two eggs, mushrooms, toast and coffee straightaway. Thank you." He then threw his voice, impersonating a waiter with a Canadian accent supposedly at the other end, "Certainly sir. Ready in fifteen minutes." We then made our way out of the washroom but hid behind a swing door to hear the Canadian gentlemen trying to order their breakfasts in English in the same way as Nev had but receiving no response, one of them took off his shoe and began hitting the air purifier with it, trying to make it work. We then beat a hasty retreat back to our rooms and we later heard that the hotel management had called a meeting of all their staff to inform them that there were a couple of eccentric Englishmen as guests in the hotel but not to panic as they were completely harmless. I think it was called the Lord Nelson hotel, a bit of a one-eyed place. On the first night of the actual show, we were both waiting in the theatre foyer for a taxi to take us back to the hotel. Nev always carried the old man dummy and props in a large silver trunk and it went everywhere with him. A very well dressed lady came across to us and asked Nev what was in the trunk. I started to make chicken noises and Nev put on a Scottish accent and it was as though the voice was from someone in the trunk. " We're a circus act, midgets and small animals." "Really?" she said as she bent down to listen. "and can you all breathe properly in there?" was her next question. Luckily for us, our taxi arrived and off we went, leaving a bewildered lady behind.We'd probably get locked up for it these days! Once back in England, we started another Black and White Minstrel Show tour and we were appearing at the Leeds Grand Theatre during the miner's strike. The theatre had to use a generator to provide lighting and one night they ran out of diesel fuel halfway through the song 'Moonlight and Roses' and the tape ran down. A stagehand gave me a torch and asked me to go out front and tell a few gags to the audience while management sent out for some more diesel fuel. The manager of the theatre came on stage and took the torch and the microphone off me and apologised to the audience, who were very understanding of the problem. "Don't believe him folks, it's always happening "I retorted. Tenor Glyn Dawson took a demijohn and went out to a petrol station down nearby Briggate, still with his black face make-up on and dressed in his red and white striped jacket, white flannels and white shoes. He scrambled out of his car and called to one of the garage attendants (this was in the days before self - service)," Hey boyo, give me a gallon of diesel for the theatre, please." The garage attendant gave him a hard stare and shouted to his mate , "Hey Harry look at this. I think we must be on Candid Camera (this was a popular TV programme of the time which featured pranks being played on the general public). I have already mentioned my love of pantomimes and I always enjoyed them. Some pantos I have been in have, shall we say, been produced on a small budget but when I was booked I never knew what kind of production it would be until I arrived for rehearsals. Billingham Forum was a lovely 1200 seater theatre in the North East, always brilliant audiences, warm and friendly people from mining or heavy industry backgrounds. I was topping the bill playing the Baron in 'Jack and the Beanstalk', not the most lavish show I had been in. I am 5ft 7in and I was bigger than the Giant who was a camp male dancer with a paper mache head. He tripped over one night and broke the nose of the head and it had to be stuck back on again. The beanstalk was a fold-up ladder with some green bunting attached and when I had to deliver the line 'here comes the beanstalk', the kids in the audience all shouted, "it's a ladder." In another panto, 'Snow White and the Seven Dwarfs'.the production company could only find five 'small people' (we have to be politically correct now!) so the five on stage shouted to the wings, "you two, stay where you are."

I did travel abroad a lot -- Egypt, Malta, Canada, America, the Far East and most European countries. Jim McDonald booked me to join an eleven week run of a 'Galaxy Show' at Jupiter's Casino on Australia's Gold Coast and we had a wonderful apartment on the beach and it was great to work in that Las Vegas - style show although one evening my act wasn't going down well at all. I was really struggling. As the house lights went up at the end of my act I saw the theatre was full of Japanese who hadn't understood a word!

12
Norman Collier
2009

Working on board cruise ships was something I looked forward to, especially so on the CANBERRA and the ARCADIA on the P and O Line and the BLACK WATCH (Fred Olsen Line) through Airtours and Seawing travel companies. It also meant that the family could join me sometimes. The first cruise I ever did was in the early 1970's and the ship's crew were all Greeks and I was asked by the Captain to put on a special show for them in their own quarters. The trouble was, not one of them spoke a word of English and an interpreter from the crew had to explain my jokes to them all. Talk about delayed action! I particularly enjoyed cruising off the eastern seaboard of America when most of the passengers would be American or Japanese but my act has always been based on visual humour, so I usually went down well --- they were a captive audience, after all! I did a two hour stint with my chicken routine, driving school sketch, stuttering microphone and club chairman pieces and various dressing up bits plus some topical gags. One cruise to the Far East included a stop - off at Jakarta when Lucy and I went onshore and for a bit of fun I did a busking act in the market place and locals threw coins into my sun hat which I had placed on the ground in anticipation. Lucy picked up the coins and used the money to buy postcards from a vendor to send home! Another time in the Bahamas, I borrowed a white jacket from the ship's Second Officer and acted out a scene from the film 'The Maltese Falcon', alternating dialogue between Sidney Greenstreet and Peter Lorre. I wasn't too sure on the night how well it had gone down with the audience and after breakfast next morning, Lucy and I ventured up to the ship's sundeck. What a nice greeting we got from a group of Americans : "Hey Elmer, look who's here. come and sit with us, Norman. Al, get these two a couple of sun loungers. Here have a Budweiser. Say, we all really enjoyed your act last night, Norman." They were great company for the rest of the cruise and we stayed in touch with them for many years.

On board I tried to do topical stuff if possible. Albert, the ship's compere, was from New York and he wrote a script for the two of us. I wore a vivid coloured dressing gown with rubber bands in my hair, my eyes were made up and I had false teeth made of orange peel, white make-up and glasses with thick lenses. My part of the script started off with "Good evening, you ladies and gentlemen. Submarine put me on board just now. Me am Mr Chu Wun Nut" -- cue Japanese - style music - "I not very athletic" and I proceeded to do a mixture of judo, Kung-Fu and other martial arts movements and then continued with the script," Acupuncture very very good for you " and I produced a large darning needle. "Compere Mr Alberto will now stick this into my arm and stamp on me to show no pain for me." Albert did pretend to do this and of course the act finished with me wincing in mock pain. Great applause from the audience and the same sort of reception on the sun deck next morning. Sam, a QC from Canada, was sunbathing with goggles on and he called across to Lucy and I, "Hey Norm, great act last night. Please come and join us for a few beers ." What a nice crowd of people they were.

Mrs Geraldo, wife of the famous band leader, was the booking agent for another cruise we signed up for and we flew out to Bangkok for a six week tour and I followed Lennie Bennett who had done the first six weeks on tour. The ship's compere Scott Peters and I dressed up as the Andrew Sisters, the great singers of the 1940's and although I hated dressing up in women's clothing, I have to admit the double act went down very well with the mainly American voyagers. The ship's captain told me that there were forty eight millionaires on board and this was in the 1970's and we had a whale of a time. On one shore visit, we saw a Canton Martial Arts Festival and a small zoo which had a couple of pandas.

In 1994 I received an invitation to present an award at the BAFTA awards held in Manchester. The show went out live on ITV and most of us were nervously waiting for our cues.George Peppard of 'A Team' fame was tap dancing on the spot as he rehearsed his lines but he was most gracious when he agreed to me having a photograph taken with him but unfortunately I never received a copy of it, despite me giving the official photographer my address. Shirley Bassey was warming her voice up prior to her singing and actor Nigel Hawthorne, who was up for a BAFTA award for his part in the film 'The Madness of King George', came across to me and introduced himself. "Now then Norman, do you know what you are doing?" he asked. I had to admit that I had no script and he seemed baffled by that but my cue came. I dashed up the wide, spiral staircase and as I came to the top of the stairs, a stagehand thrust a microphone into my hands and I was away, did a couple of quick gags and handed over the award to the Soundmen Crew of the Year and came off-stage and went back down into the basement where Nigel was talking to Dickie Attenborough and he broke off to greet me with the acclamation, "Norman, you were absolutely wonderful out there. Well done." Princess Anne was guest for the evening but I didn't fancy being snubbed by her for a second time.

Throughout my life, and even before I turned professional, I have always wanted to make people laugh. It's a wonderful feeling seeing and hearing the laughter from a supportive audience and certainly makes up for the odd times I have come off - stage to the sound of my own footsteps, having 'died the death', However, talking to fellow comedians over the years, we have all had that happen to us, even that great comedy duo Eric Morecombe and Ernie Wise were not particularly successful until they got their big chance on television and they never looked back. Their years of experience in clubs and variety theatres throughout the country stood them in good stead when they made the big time. Our paths never crossed but they were big favourites of mine.I suppose my style of comedy was mainly simple. I rarely worked from a script, relying on the visual stuff which seemed to go down well and I liked to ad lib with an audience and 'play it off the cuff'. Of course that was never possible on television shows where the Producer was in complete charge and his or her word was gospel. A four or five minute spot had to be exactly that and woe betide anyone who didn't stick to the show script. I'm not too sure how they got Ken Dodd to conform though! Doddy and I have always got on well together and I have been sat next to him on top tables at various dinners and he has spent the entire night scribbling ideas and jokes in his notebook. He has always been supportive of me if he has been in the audience at one of my shows and has popped into my dressing room afterwards for a natter. We had a laugh when I took Lucy and her friend Brenda Wileman backstage at Hull New Theatre when Ken had topped the bill. He was sat in vest and long johns in his dressing room and we all had a drink and a chat when he stood up and asked the ladies if they would turn round as he wanted to get changed. They did as requested but found themselves facing a full length mirror and Ken smiling back at them. Earlier in his show that night, a wag on the front row shouted out to Ken that him and his wife had a taxi home booked for 11pm. Quick as a flash, Ken replied, "Why, are you leaving at the interval?" The length of his shows are legendary and I am sure that theatre stagehands all over the country groaned when their theatres booked a Ken Dodd Special, knowing that they would not be leaving until the early hours of the morning when he appeared but what great value Ken has given over the years and I was delighted to hear that Richard Madeley and Judy Finnigan had launched an appeal on their 'Richard and Judy' show on Channel Four TV to have Ken knighted. Good luck, 'Sir'Ken --- your knighthood would be well deserved. I usually enjoyed appearing on television and Les Dawson was responsible for inviting me to appear on BBC TV's show 'Blankety Blank' in 1988 when he was a regular compere of the show. Guests were put up at a hotel near to the television studios in Wood Lane, London and two shows were recorded in the one day. We all had a chat before the recordings on who was to sit where but very little rehearsal and we had no idea of programme content but I enjoyed the experience when Les or Terry Wogan were in charge. I also enjoyed meeting up with Hull-born Joe Longthorne, athlete Tessa Sanderson, Vince Hill, Anne Robinson and Wendy Richard at the shows as well as Lena Zavaroni whose death was so sad because she was such a lovely girl with a natural talent. She was like a schoolgirl running round the tv studio and I first met her in the early 1970's when we shared the same management, Dorothy Solomon.

Les Dawson and I hit it off straightaway the first time we were on the ITV programme 'Let's Laugh' and we kept in touch and I was as pleased as punch when Les and his first wife Meg invited me to be godfather at their daughter's christening. They lived in a semi detached house in Whitefield, Bury and whenever Lucy and I were invited round for a meal, Les and I would always wash the pots up afterwards and he would speak in his W C Fields' voice, "Well Norm?, how did you enjoy the meal tonight?" and this sort of patter went on until all the pots, pans and utensils had been washed, dried and put away. God knows what anyone listening would have made of our conversation! Les's act then consisted of him playing the piano and telling a few gags. Now, my home city of Hull can lay claim to changing the whole style of his performances. He was appearing at the St Andrew's Club off Hessle Road and his act had not gone down particularly well. The trawler men and their wives gave Les a hard time and threw beer mats at him on stage. He had to do a second spot later that night, much to the packed audience's obvious dislike. He was so fed up that he had had a good drink in his dressing room during the bingo interval and went back on stage, determined to get his own back with the hecklers and he deliberately insulted them throughout his act, pulling all sorts of strange faces and playing the piano off-key. Surprise, surprise. The audience gave Les a standing ovation at the end of his act and he decided there and then to change his style of entertaining and success was just around the corner for him. I saw Les in panto in Leeds --- 'Babes in the Wood' with Eli Wood. Don Revie, the former Leicester City, Hull City and Manchester City footballer and then manager of Leeds United was in the audience. His club were playing well for him at the time but the goalkeeper Gary Sprake had been under pressure in some recent games. Les came on stage with a sack slung over his shoulder and Eli asked, "what have you got in the sack?" "Gary Sprake's head" replied Les to a mixed chorus of boos, jeers and cheers.

Throughout my career, I have often been asked for advice by aspiring comedians. I always advise them to look for things other's do not see. Modern comics would never ask us oldies for advice -- it's a totally different world now. I have never thought much of swearing and vulgarity to get a few cheap laughs. Modern comedy is a bit too dark for me but then I suppose modern life is dark. Nowadays, television is all - powerful and omni - present and working men's clubs belong to another era but it does mean comics miss out on learning their trade thoroughly through years of experience but tv is a hard taskmaster and comedy material is soon used up, so insatiable is television. That's my opinion anyway, for what it's worth. My chicken routine and stuttering microphone act have become my trademark over the years although I haven't always been happy to become so typecast but producers and the public have insisted I keep them in my act. Barney Colehan, producer of BBC TV's 'The Good Old Days', always wanted me to include my chicken routine, as did Bruce Forsyth. I had done this routine on BBC's 'The Generation Game' in 1994 when Jim Davidson stepped in briefly for Bruce and when I appeared on the show again later that year with Bruce back as compere, he said to me at rehearsals, "Now Norman, you've got to do your chicken act because it went down very well with the audience and the viewers last time." How could I refuse Brucie?! If I haven't included it when I have been appearing, I have been stopped by disappointed theatre goers afterwards asking me why I hadn't done it, so who am I to judge? Most British comedians over the years have developed a trademark style or saying. Look at Jimmy Wheeler (Aye, Aye, that's your lot), Al Read (Reight Monkey), Norman Wisdom (cloth cap and short jacket), Tommy Trinder (You lucky people), Max Miller (The Cheeky Chappie), Dick Emery (Oh,you are awful), Charlie Williams (Now then, me old flower), Max Bygraves (I wanna tell you a story), Bruce Forsyth (Nice to see you, to see you, nice), Jim Bowen (Bullseye), Frankie Howard (Oh, missus), Arthur Askey (Hello playmates), Nat Jackley (Rubberneck), Duncan Norvelle (Chase me, chase me), Sandy Powell (Can you hear me, mother?), Norman Evans (Over the garden wall), Tommy Cooper (Red fez and Just like that). I first met Ken Dodd when I was appearing in the Cabaret Club in Liverpool and he was in the audience. After the show he bought me a beer, it was a privilege to meet him. My own favourites are many and varied --- Roy Hudd and Barry Cryer are my type of comics as were Chic Murray, Jimmy James and Roy Castle, Bob Monkhouse and Alfred Marks. Albert Modley made me laugh but I don't know what audiences in the south of England made of his broad Lancashire accent. Jimmy Edwards, Tony Hancock, Jimmy Clitheroe, Joe Gladwin, Frank Randle, Bernard Manning, Frank Carson, Roy Walker, Mike Reid, Ronnie Corbett, Russ Abbot, Arthur Lucan (Old Mother Riley), who actually died in the wings waiting to go on at Hull's Tivoli Theatre on 17 May 1954, aged 69 and he is buried in Hull's Eastern Cemetery on Preston Road. A bust of him is in a baker's shop on the site of the Tivoli, which was demolished in 1957; Spike Milligan, Harry Secombe, Ronnie Barker, Cannon and Ball, Flanagan and Allen, Freddie Starr, although he wasn't popular with the Laurie Holloway band when he covered them with foam at one show I shared the billing with him. From across the Atlantic, I always admired the timing and sheer talents of Bob Hope, George Burns, Jack Benny, Stan Laurel and Oliver Hardy and The Three Stooges and Abbott and Costello. Wow, just writing all these names down has made me laugh out loud with memories of their individual humour. I remember appearing in London with Roger de Courcey and Nookie, his bear and Freddie 'Parrot Face' Davies and the three of us were sharing a dressing room when Norman Vaughan, compere of the show, popped his head round the door and muttered, "I'm glad I'm not sharing this dressing room with all this chicken, parrot and bear s*** all over the floor." My friend Norman Wisdom was always full of mischief. On one occasion I was sat next to him at a Water Rats Charity Lunch and he dipped his finger into my soup, sucked it and informed me that my soup was cold. He then acted the fool throughout the meal. He had a great talent which showed in the popular films he made which I loved. I first met Eric Sykes during a summer season in Blackpool when he invited the stars of the various shows to a late meal in Yates Wine Lodge and we have been good friends ever since. It gave me great pleasure in later years when he told me he considered me to be 'the comedian's comedian.' What an accolade from a great man but how on earth could I live up to that? I am also indebted to Eric because he once introduced me to Sean Connery 'Mr James Bond', when we shared a table at a charity dinner, another moment when the little labourer from Hull couldn't quite believe who he was sat with. I met Scottish comic Stanley Baxter in the canteen at London Weekend Television after I filmed a show with Russ Abbot. Stanley had a bun and a cup of tea on his tray and I remember he was wearing a brown cardigan with holes in the sleeves. I sat down along side him and introduced myself. He told me he was rehearsing a Bonnie Langford take - off for a show scheduled to be televised the next weekend. What a nice gentleman he was. My real favourite comic though was Max Wall, known as 'The Professor' in his black tights, black boots and long, black wig, playing the piano, guitar and singing. What a superb craftsman Max was, funny walk and all. I once saw him on stage at Hull's Palace Theatre and I adored his brilliance and timing. Freddie Sales from Hull made me laugh. He had a hilarious act involving him dressed up as a baby in a pram, nappy and dummy included. Billy Dainty was a fellow Water Rat and another big favourite of mine with his seemingly rubber legs and very funny balloon dance. I shared the bill once with Arthur English at the Scala Club in Doncaster. He was a typical spiv, with a loud, check suit and gaudy tie and he had a thin, black moustache which he used to pencil on in the dressing room.'Open the cage, play the music' were the words he always finished his act with. Mick Miller with his 'Guzzlers Gin' drunken act made me roar with laughter as did Dickie Henderson and Freddie Frinton from

Cleethorpes with his 'Dinner For One' act.The Marx Brothers were not really my cup of tea but the Three Stooges certainly were. In the main, I didn't find women comedians very funny but I did admire Hylda Baker, Tessie O'Shea, Marti Caine and Lucille Ball. Appearing live on TISWAS, a Saturday morning kids TV programme with presenter Chris Tarrant and black comic Lenny Henry was a hoot. It was around the time of a television programme ROOTS about African slaves and Lenny and I devised a slapstick sketch around the programme. He came out of a tent, wailing "Where's my roots, where's my roots?" I then appeared, dressed in an AA uniform with a street map in my hand and the comment" Now which routes would you like, sir?" I met superstar Phil Collins through this programme and we shared the same sense of humour.

Ron Cousins was Head of Entertainment at Eastbourne and we knew each other from when he was manager of the Alhambra Theatre in Bradford and before that when he looked after the ABC Theatre in my home city of Hull. Ron had booked me to appear for a summer season in Eastbourne along with comedy duo Little and Large. I was playing golf with Eddie Large at the Royal Golf Club in the town on our day off and two ladies come towards us from an adjoining fairway. The larger of the two ladies addressed Eddie with the question, "Excuse me, but are you sure you're playing the right ball?" Eddie's ball had his name printed on it so he was sure he hadn't played the wrong ball and told the lady this. "Oh, you're that entertainer Eddie Large, aren't you? I've never found you to be very funny." she replied, before walking off and as she passed me, I doffed my cap and said, "and I'm Syd Little, Eddie's partner." "I know that" she sniffed and the two ladies continued looking for their golf balls as Eddie and I looked to the skies. Happy memories. Eddie and Syd have continued to be my great friends throughout my career, They are Godfathers to Karen and John's eldest son Jonathan, now 28. They have both continued to be friends of our family with their wives Sherrie and Patsy. Wonderful memories of lovely people and lovely times together. There was a sort of 'comedians union' and we swapped jokes in some cases and generally supported each other's efforts including stories of appearing at theatres such as first house at the Glasgow Empire on a wet Monday night in January. However, it's a fact that not all comedians like Syd and Eddie are as funny off-stage. I never liked watching myself on tv as I was very critical of my performance and I suppose that's still the case these days.

13

Norman Collier

2009

For the past twenty years or so, people have been asking me when I am going to retire from show business. I say when the telephone stops ringing. Charities are very dear to my heart and I try to help whenever I can. The Variety Club of Great Britain (Merseyside and North Wales Committee) organised a Millenium Charity Show and I joined Ricky Tomlinson, The Merseybeats, Jimmy Cricket, Jimmy James and the Vagabonds and the Black Abbots in performing. I joined hundreds of tap dancing, high kicking youngsters crossing the Humber Bridge as part of BBC Radio Humberside's Christmas Charity Appeal. The plan was that I would walk with them for a mile or so and then get on board the BBC bus which was following us. Unfortunately, strong side winds caused the bridge to be closed to high-sided vehicles and so I had no choice but to walk the three miles across the bridge and back but we did raise £4,500 for the appeal which made it all worthwhile. I was invited to switch on the 2004 Christmas Lights in Barton upon Humber, a thriving little town just across the river from Hull and the same week I played Scrooge in a pantomime in Hessle which was written by Joey Howard and my son-in-law John Ainsley also starred in it and we all had some laughs at rehearsals and during the shows. In the winter of 2006, I toured 17 venues in England with Frank Carson, Duncan Norvelle and Ian 'Sludge' Lee and we played to full houses at smaller theatres on a really enjoyable tour. Frank has been a good pal of mine for years. We played summer seasons at Blackpool North Pier and Great Yarmouth. Lucy and I have had some good times with Frank and his wife Ruth and we shared the same agent at one time, Dorothy Solomon. We were flying back to Blackpool on a private plane after a Sunday evening show on the South Coast, along with The Bachelors singing group. Frank fell asleep almost as soon as we were airborne and laid there snoring with his mouth wide open. His son Tony made us all laugh with the comment, "Gentlemen, enjoy the semi - silence while you can ." Venues for our 2006 tour were mainly in the Midlands and along the south coast and they were organised by Brian Yates Associates and compered by comedian Paul Adams.

Stephen Smith is a criminal lawyer from Rotherham in South Yorkshire and he is also a best - selling author of some very amusing books, describing incidents which have occurred during his working life. Stephen has also written the life story of Charlie Williams from his days as an old fashioned centre half with Doncaster Rovers in the old Division Three (North) up to the highlights of Charlie's career as a comic after his success on Yorkshire Television's show 'The Comedians'. Stephen has also compered some of my one man shows in Barnsley and Rotherham which feature a chat for an hour and then cabaret for the next hour.

It's been a very rewarding experience for me looking back and I am very grateful to my wife Lucy and all my family for their tremendous support over the years. I also owe a big debt of gratitude to those fans who have stayed loyal to me during my career ----thanks to both of them.

14

Norman Collier

2009

I compered a Sunday concert in Skegness when the stars of the show were the American singing sensations, the Everly Brothers --- Don and Phil --- both great guys whose hit records included 'Dream, Dream, Dream', 'Wake Up, Little Susie', 'Til I kissed yer' and 'Bye, Bye Love'. I had arrived at the theatre, not knowing what was exactly expected of me and I went straight to the boys dressing room, knocked on the door and introduced myself to them. Don was strumming a Gibson guitar in the corner of the room and Phil was having a kip on the sofa. Just to make polite conversation, I remarked to Don what a nice guitar it was. "Do you want it, Norman?" he asked, "here take it. It's a Gibson but I've got a couple more in the bus". I politely refused his generous offer but if I had accepted, how much would it be worth now, especially if the two brothers had signed it?

As I sit in my bungalow, just ten miles from where I was born and now in my 84th year, I count my blessings. How lucky I have been to have such a long career doing what I have always loved doing, making people laugh. I never wanted fame, chased celebrity or wished to be a star. My pleasure and privilege was hearing the laughter. I have met some wonderful people along the way. Lucy and I have been married more than sixty years and we see our son, daughters, daughter-in-law, sons-in-law, grandchildren and great-grandchildren most days and laughter plays a big part in all our lives and it really is the best medicine ! My career was always second to the family. It was just a job but what a job!

When I was checking out my old diaries, I realised just how much television I had done and I will forever be grateful to the BBC and ITV production teams. Here are just some of my television and appearances together with some more highlights which I will hope will bring some happy memories to readers:

TELEVISION 1966 David Nixon's Comedy Bandbox (Three times)

1970 Tintin et Les Oranges Blueues

1971 The Royal Command Variety performance

1972 Ten appearances in 'Jokers Wild', Saturday Variety Show

1973 Thirteen appearances in 'Jokers Wild', Junior Showtime - 'Babes in the Wood'

1974 'Wheeltappers and Shunters Social Club', 'Look Who's Talking'.

1975 'Lulu show' with Labbi Siffre, Bernie Clifton, The Shadows. I sang 'We'll Gather Lilacs'. 'Look Who's Talking.'

1976 Three appearances on 'Joker's Wild'. 'The Good Old Days' with Barbara Windsor, Valerie Masterson, Jan Hunt and members of the Players Theatre, London. 'The Little and Large Telly show.' 'Look Who's Talking' with Derek Batey,

1978 'Weymouth Seaside Special' with John Inman, Hope and Keen, Lenny Henry, Bobby Crush, Salena Jones, Elaine Carroll, Barry Howard, Dana Gillespie, Raymond Bowers and First Edition. 'Larry Grayson's Generation Game' with Rolf Harris, Windsor Davies and Don Estelle, Lennie Bennett, Clive Dunn, David Hamilton, Tony Blackburn, Frank Thomton, Bill Pertwee, John Inman, Isla St. Clair.

Christrnas Day 1978. My 53rd birthday,

'Larry Grayson's Generation Game' with Isla St. Clair, Jon Pertwee, Mollie Sugden, Gerald Harper, Ian Cuthbertson, Eric Sykes, Terry Wogan, Barbara Windsor, Norman Vaughn, Esther Rantzen, Freddie "Parrot Face"

Davies, Roger de Courcey and Marti Caine. I did my 'Laughing Soldier' routine.

1979 Five 'Freddie Starr's Variety Madhouse', 'Tiswas'.

1980 'Michael Parkinson Show' with John Arlott and Emlyn Willliams. Not a very enjoyable show for me.

'Larry Grayson's Generation Game' with Kenneth McKellar, Keith Chegwin and Maggie Philbin, Roy Hudd and Cyril Fletcher. 'Des O'Connor Tonight' with Ken Dodd, Mimi Hines. I performed the song 'Two Little Boys'. 'Russ Abbot's Madhouse' - four shows; 'Tiswas', 'Jokers Wild', 'Blankety Blank' (twice). '3-2-I' Music Hall'. 'Russell Harty Show', Sandy Powell ("can you hear me, mother?") and I performed a panto sketch.

1981 'Larry Grayson's Generation Game', Little and Large, Reg Varney, Tom O'Connor, Aimi Macdonald and Elaine Stritch. 'Larry Grayson's Generation Game', Isla St. Clair, Cyril Fletcher, Dilys Watling, James Smillie, Anna Dawson, Johnny Vyuyan, Tony Hart. 'Lena Zavaroni Show' with Nana Mouskouri. 'Brighton Summertime Special' with Lulu, Vince Hill and Showaddywaddy. 'Blankety - Blank', 'Punchlines' (two shows) 'Hi There 82!' Hi-Di-Hi team, Diana Dors, Danny La Rue, Andy Williams,Wall Street Crash, Kenny Ball and his Jazzmen.

1982 'Eastboume Summertime Special', Shirley Bassey, Bemie Clifton, Stutz Bear Cats, 'Blankety - Blank', 'Look Who's Talking', 'Russell Harty Show - Alan Lake and Diana Dors, Victoria Wood, Molly Keane, Brian Robson, Julie Walters, The Great Soprendo. This show was shot in Russell Harty's home in North Yorkshire and I talked to him about digs I had stayed in, blew up an inflatable doll and I sang 'Soldiers of the Queen' as it slowly deflated.

1983 'Blankety - Blank' with Terry Wogan, Joe Brown, Lynsey de Paul, Gloria Hunniford, Danny La Rue and Wendy Richard. 'Jim Davidson

Special', 'Entertainment Express', 'Punchlines' (four shows).

1984 'Marti Caine Special' with Alan Price and Pat Coombs. 'The Saturday Picture Show' with Mark Curry, Maggie Philbin, Peter Powell, Nick Beggs of Kajagoogoo, David Copperfield. 'The Main Attraction' Duncan Norvelle, David Copperfield, Gary Numan, Lulu, Deniece Williams, Max Wall. 'Punchlines' (three shows). 'Live from Her Majesty's', 'English Resource Units' 11-13: Speech! 'A Century of Stars - The Story of the Grand Order of Water Rats.

1985 'The Little and Large Show' with The Drifters and Geoffrey Hughes. 'An Evening with Dennis Taylor'

1986 I've no idea what happened this year!

1987 'Tom O'Connor Roadshow' with Westworld, Guy Ingle, Patrick Strong and the Cambridge University Rowing Team. 'Blankety - Blank' with Les Dawson, Geoff Capes, Bella Emberg, Rula Lenska, Diana Sheridan and Dennis Waterman. Led 500 people dancing the Can Can across the Humber Bridge (the longest suspension bridge in the world) to raise funds to buy mini buses for the disabled. 'Live from the Palladium' 'Summertime Special' '3-2-1 Christrnas Special' 'Switch on of Hull's Christmas Lights'

1988 'Mr H is late' 'Blankety - Blank' with Les Dawson, Vince Hill, Joe Longthome, Wendy Richard, Anne Robinson and Tessa Sanderson. 'Breakfast Time TV' - Landladies charrn. John Stapleton interviewed me about my experiences with landladies.

1989 & 1990 Don't know where I was in these years!

1991 Harry Gration interviewed me on the death of Barney Colehan who started up 'The Good Old Days' on TV from the Leeds City Varieties. Roy Hudd, Ken Dodd and Les Dawson also featured.

1992 Must have been on the high seas on the cruise liners !

1993 'The Paul Daniels Magic Show' with Debbie McGee, Jim Bowen,

John Inman, Ruth Madoc, Carmen Silvera, Marty Feldman.

1994 Peter Levy previews the (brief) return of the Good Old Days to the Leeds City Varieties with Les Dawson. I was interviewed in the theatre itself. 'Bruce Forsyth's Generation Game' (but hosted by Jim Davidson) with Rosemarie Ford. Frank Carson and I were game judges. 'Bruce Forsyth's Generation Game' with Bruce and Rosemarie Ford, Frank Bruno and Johnny Morris. 'Cryer's Crackers' with Barry Cryer

1995 'Talking Telephone Numbers' I also featured in other shows including The Grimleys, It's George Jones and the Barrymore Show. I haven't done a great deal of radio over the years, apart from interviews, because my style has always been visual but four shows I was involved in bring back happy memories for me:- Windsor Davies presents......with Mike Reid and Rory McGrath, Vince Hill's Solid Gold Music Show with Amalda Bancroft, The Grumbleweeds with Peter Skellern and The 50th Anniversary of the Good Old Days when Barry Cryer presented soundclips of myself, Eartha Kitt, Arthur Askey and Morecombe and Wise.